THE

BUFFALO

NEW YORK

Cookbook

FROM THE "NICKEL CITY"

70

RECIPES

THE BUFFALO
NEW YORK

Cookbook

★ ARTHUR BOVINO ★

The Countryman Press

A division of W. W. Norton & Company

Independent Publishers Since 1923

For information about permission to reproduce selections from this book, write to
Permissions, The Countryman Press, 500 Fifth Avenue, New York, NY 10110

For information about special discounts for bulk purchases, please contact
W. W. Norton Special Sales at specialsales@wwnorton.com or 800-233-4830

Manufacturing by Versa Press
Book design by Lidija Tomas
Production manager: Devon Zahn

Names: Bovino, Arthur, 1976– author.
Title: The Buffalo New York cookbook : 70 recipes from the "Nickel City" / Arthur Bovino.
Description: New York, NY : Countryman Press, a division of W. W. Norton & Company
Independent Publishers Since 1923, [2018] | Includes index.
Identifiers: LCCN 2018036643 | ISBN 9781682683231 (pbk.)
Subjects: LCSH: Cooking, American. | Cooking—New York—Buffalo. | LCGFT: Cookbooks.
Classification: LCC TX715 B758 2018 | DDC 641.59747/97—dc23
LC record available at https://lccn.loc.gov/2018036643

The Countryman Press
www.countrymanpress.com

A division of W. W. Norton & Company, Inc.
500 Fifth Avenue, New York, NY 10110
www.wwnorton.com

978-1-68268-323-1 (pbk.)

10 9 8 7 6 5 4 3 2

To my son, Augustus, my wife, Angela, my family, friends, and the people of Western New York. Buffalove.

CONTENTS

Introduction 9

A Note About Recipes, Equipment, and Ingredients 12

WINGS 17

Buffalo Wing Sauce 22

Old-School Buffalo Wings 23

Baked Buffalo Wings 29

Chef Marshal Grady's Bleu Bayou Wings 33

Elmo's Cajun-Barbecue Wings 36

Homemade Blue Cheese Dressing (for Wings) . . 38

Homemade Hot Sauce 40

Off-the-Pit BBQ Buffalo Wings 44

Red Sox Wing Sauce
    (Garlic Parmesan Hot Wings) 45

Spicy Blue Cheese Buffalo Sauce 46

Whirl Wing Sauce 47

BEEF ON WECK 49

Homemade Kummelweck Rolls 50

Beef on Weck Roast Beef 52

Easy Homemade Horseradish 53

Easy Beef on Weck 54

BUFFALO FAMOUS: Other Iconic Buffalo Dishes (a.k.a. Food Buffalebrities) 59

Buffalo Pizza Dough 62

Buffalo Pizza Sauce 62

Buffalo Pizza 62

Chicken Finger Sub 64

Fish Fry 65

Fried Bologna Sandwich 67

Lottie's Pierogi and Buffalo Wing Pierogi 70

Oliver's Spinach Loaf 72

Pasta con Sarde 75

Pizza Logs 78

Spaghetti Parm (Meatballs and Sausage Not
    Included) 80

Buffalo Stinger Taco 83

Stuffed Banana Peppers 86

Ted's Hot Dog Relish 87

Sponge Candy 90

Tom & Jerry Cocktail 93

BUFFALO "BASICS" 95

Blue Cheese Sour Cream 95

Buffalo-ized Bacon 97

Buffalo Bread Crumbs 98

Buffalo Panko 98

Buffalo Refried Beans 99

Homemade Mayonnaise
(and Buffalo Mayo) 100

Shredded Buffalo Chicken (Instant Pot, Oven-
Roasted, Poached/Stovetop, Slow Cooker) . . 101

BUFFALO THIS, BUFFALO THAT, BUFFALO EVERYTHING 105

Buffalo Wings and Blue Cheese
Buttermilk Waffles 107

Buffalo Chicken Grilled
Cheese Sandwich 109

Buffalo Chicken Pot Pie 111

Speed Metal Fries 113

Buffalo Fried Rice 116

Buffalo Chicken Mac & Cheese 117

Buffalo Salmon 118

Buffalo Wedge Salad 121

Primanti Sandwich, Buffalo-Style 122

Cream of Buffalo Wing Soup 124

RINGS, STICKERS & OTHER APPS. 127

Broccoli and Cauliflower "Wings" 128

Buffalo Chicken Bacon Biscuit Bombs 130

Blue Cheese Buffalo Deviled Eggs 131

Buffalo Rock Shrimp with
Blue Cheese Tempura 133

Buffalo Potstickers 135

Cheesy Buffalo Chicken Ring 136

Twice-Baked Buffalo Wing Potatoes 138

ADDICTIVE BUFFALO-IZED PARTY DIPS & DISHES 141

Buffalo 7-Layer Dip 143

Buffalo Chicken Casserole 144

Buffalo Chicken Nachos 146

Buffalo Chicken Parm "Pizza" 149

Buffalo Chicken Pimento Cheese Salad 151

Buffalo Queso 152

Buffalo Chicken Sloppy Joes
(a.k.a. Buffalo Joes) 153

Buffalo Chip Dip 155

Buffalo Coleslaw (Buffaslaw) 157

DAYTRIP DISHES 159

Chesterfield–Style Chicken Riggies 160

Grape Pie 162

Robert Baker–Style Cornell
Barbecue Chicken 165

Utica Greens 166

Acknowledgments 169

Index 171

INTRODUCTION

Wings are huge in Buffalo. Obviously. But they're not the only thing the city has going for it, food-wise. Not by a longshot. That's something I knew anecdotally, but didn't fully comprehend until I spent a month in the city eating at more than 120 of its most well-known and beloved restaurants. While eating and interviewing its chefs, food bloggers, writers, bartenders, and restaurateurs, I collected what I learned in a book called *Buffalo Everything: A Guide to Eating in the Nickel City*. It details more in-depth wing lore than you can wag a drumstick at, and goes into the origins of its other iconic foods, including beef on weck, Buffalo–style pizza, Tom & Jerry cocktails, sponge candy, stingers, chicken finger subs, and more. If you're looking for the best places to find those icons, that book provides the lists, grist, and context for understanding the people and history behind them.

Consider *this* as both standalone cookbook and kitchen companion guide to the first volume, complete with some 70 recipes.

The book is basically divided into two portions. The first covers the city's actual iconic foods. And sure—that means wings. You'll learn how to make them the way they're made in Buffalo, the secrets to a great wing sauce and buttermilk blue cheese dressing, and discover a little about why it's difficult to find ones that are truly equal elsewhere. Additionally, there are preparations that *aren't* as well-known outside Buffalo (like off-the-pit wings), and a few truly special and addictive ones that aren't even as well-known *there* (like Elmo's Cajun wings and the hot garlic Parmesan "Red Sox" or "stinky" wings served at Wiechec's and Bases Loaded).

And that doesn't even touch on the "secret" butter substitute some spots use or the recipe for

Chef Marshal Grady's "Bleu Bayou Wings" served two hours east of Buffalo at Abigail's in Waterloo, NY, which were named the world's best by director Matt Reynolds and his group of experts after visiting more than 70 wing spots for his film, *The Great Chicken Wing Hunt.*

This first part of this book also explains, in depth, how to make Buffalo's other and lesser-known food icons, with recipes based on firsthand experiences eating at Buffalo's most storied places, as well as interviews with the city's most respected chefs, writers, and restaurateurs. These are dishes from across Buffalo's culinary spectrum—from fried bologna to spaghetti Parm—many of which originated from various immigrant populations and continue on today to defy cultural boundaries, helping define the city's blue-collar, comfort-food cuisine.

The second portion of this book is a testament to the culinary viral force that *is* Buffalo "flavor."

When it comes to Buffalo-izing America's favorite foods, there really are few limitations. Buffalo flavor is something the folks who come up with fast-food menus and snack food flavors have gotten increasingly savvy about. After taking over chicken and bar menus, and finding its way onto tables at international chains like TGI Fridays, McDonald's, and Pizza Hut, this classic flavor has become ubiquitous and gone way beyond wings, Buffalo-izing a dizzying number of other commercially successful products. There are Buffalo potato chips, Buffalo chicken nuggets, Buffalo and blue cheese cheese curls, pretzels, popcorn, cheese (Cheddar, Monterey, curds), Doritos, dips, and sauces. There's even Buffalo wing soda!

And while *true* Buffalo flavor tastes like Paula's doughnuts, fried bologna at The Pink at two in the morning, chargrilled hot dogs at Ted's, and beef on weck at Schwabl's, it's hard to argue with the effect of applying the flavor profile to many of America's other favorite dishes. I would know. In the process of my research, I went from writing a cookbook to writing a guide book, and, eventually, to writing both. There was just too much to eat and too much to write about. In fact, in the process, the eating and writing almost became a compulsion. There came a day, after Buffalo-izing everything from bread crumbs and bacon to salmon and chicken Parm, when I had to look in the mirror and just say, "You have to stop."

There are things I'm sure you can't Buffalo-ize. But I struggle to think of them. And it's not like I didn't have some failures along the way. (Trust me when I say that no matter what you've read or seen online, you don't want to line your tube pan with blue cheese dressing when making monkey bread.) But nothing that failed left me with the thought that it couldn't work if just done differently. In fact, if you suggest something you think *wouldn't* work, go ahead, try—Caesar salad, caramels, cotton candy, ice cream? I bet they would— the wheels start turning. I just begin thinking about ways they *could*.

Which leads me to explain—before we jump into the ingredients and equipment you might want to check to see if you have (none of it too expensive or fancy)—what I mean about Buffalo-izing, and a few insights about the best ways to go about it.

There is, of course, the urge to *just add Frank's* to things. There's a whole advertising campaign based on this school of thought: Ethel's "I put that @$%& on everything!" And while I keep at least one bottle of Frank's in the fridge on a shelf with some 20 other hot sauces, and several more bottles in the pantry, I don't fully buy into it. Not only does using Frank's not do justice to Buffalo and the original inspiration (wings, obviously) for Buffalo-*izing*, but it just

doesn't always help pull off the homage. You want that classic flavor, but adding other ingredients to round it out will frankly (pun intended) make dishes more impressive and delicious. Poblanos, jalapeños, and other hot peppers (seeds removed if you're cooking for the timid) will add depth of flavor.

The other thing is that some dishes can carry the flavor but don't have the classic crunch or crispiness of fried wings. When there are ways to reintroduce that texture—to mac and cheese, for example with Buffalo-ized bacon—you can deliciously echo the original wing. And while you're looking for ways to riff on the wings' texture and flavor, also consider how to employ the iconic accompanying condiments in ways that both call up or reinterpret the original dish, but without forcing it. This all helps bring home the theme.

One of the things everyone loves about wings, once they hear the tale, is the eureka moment of their inception, that ingenuity inherent in Teressa Bellissimo's original dish. Haven't heard the well-worn story? Frank and Teressa Bellissimo owned a bar, and late one Friday night, their son and his hungry friends tumbled in. Teressa needed to come up with something on the fly and had some chicken wings on hand that she was going to use to make a soup. Instead, she fried them up and tossed them in hot sauce mixed with butter. The story is potentially a lot more nuanced, but the rest, as they say, is wing-story. And regardless of what happened in that kitchen, the spirit of the moment lives on: part of Buffalo-izing a dish in a way that echoes the original and creates something that stands on its own is to look for ways to channel that original energy.

Are there ways to integrate all the components of the original (wings/chicken, Frank's RedHot, butter, celery, blue cheese dressing, and sometimes carrots) into whatever you're "Buffalo-izing" naturally? Look for dishes where they're all organically there to be riffed on. Chicken soup and chicken pot pie already have chicken and the matching vegetables and creamy bases. Both are natural fits for being Buffalo-ized. Many of our favorite comfort foods, while they have nothing to do with Buffalo wings (just chicken wings in Buffalo), are also natural fits for the flavor riff. Mac and cheese, grilled cheese, deviled eggs, you name it. Consider these kinds of dishes.

Regarding cheats: I'm not going to lie and tell you I've never in my life used a store-bought dressing or premade sauce and that you shouldn't either. Typically, for me, cheats happen when I run out of the batches I prepared in advance while hosting. (Always keep a few bottles of Frank's and blue cheese dressing as backup.)

I can tell you that at least when it comes to those essentials, it's super easy to make them from scratch—we're talking 10 to 15 minutes to make wing sauce (two parts melted butter to three parts Frank's) and blue cheese dressing. They're going to taste better and they may even be better for you. Check out the ingredients in butter substitutes and bottled dressings if you don't believe me.

If you are going to cheat, be smart about how, in your own way. I won't make my own puff pastry for pot pie (though I'd advise making your own crust unless you're in a rush) or wonton wrappers for Buffalo potstickers, but biscuits (for bacon bombs) and salsa (if you're going that route with your nachos)? Just make them yourself—it's easy. And at the same time as I'd say cut your own fries, I typically don't shred my own hash browns and I think there's something beautiful about making queso with Velveeta and Ro-Tel.

Which is all to say, if you want to use canned refried beans and think it's crazy to include a recipe for making your own flour tortillas from scratch in a book that tells you how to remake a fast-food taco (Colosso's "Stinger") at home, I hear you.

Here are two pieces of advice I would encourage you to follow, though. The first is to just go ahead and keep a quart container (or half-quart container) of both wing sauce and blue cheese dressing in your fridge as you embark on these recipes. It will make the process easier if you don't have to make the sauces over and over again, and so, your Buffalo-izing will be all the more enjoyable. The other piece of advice? Have fun, throw out the rules, and be comfortable getting crazy with your ideas and inspirations.

Hey, after all, it worked for Teressa.

A NOTE ABOUT RECIPES, EQUIPMENT, AND INGREDIENTS

The recipes in this book are the results of interviews, and reworking old recipes found in articles and books in the research library of the Buffalo History Museum and online. While a few recipes may be tricky (here's looking at you, Kummelweck), most are fairly straightforward and don't require any special equipment beyond a large pot and a thermometer.

That being said, if you're at all serious about making great wings, let's just get this out of the way: you probably want to invest in a small kitchen fryer.

You'll find all kinds of articles online that talk about the best way to cook the crispiest wings. Par-frying, brining, air-drying overnight in the fridge, rice flour . . . there are debatable merits to all of these techniques. The truth is that the key to great wings is *frying* at the right temperature for as much time as they need. That's it! The easiest way to do that? That small kitchen fryer.

You *can* use a Dutch oven or any big high-edged pot and a candy and deep-fry stainless-steel thermometer (I recommend the accurate, durable, and easy-to-clean one my friend, Chef Tom Woodbury, turned me onto: the Thermapen made by Thermo-Works). The recipes in this book that require frying will tell you what temperature to get your oil to. But between having to monitor and adjust the temperature of the oil on the stove, the mess even a covered pot full of boiling oil is going to create, keeping track of cooking times, and coordinating all of the above while playing host—which, let's face it, you're probably going to be doing if you're taking the time to make wings—you're going to make better wings more safely and have more fun doing it if you just buy a fryer.

Think about it this way: some of the best foods are fried foods, and if you're making wings, fries and fish fry probably aren't far behind. The good news is that you can find a good fryer online for under $50. I use a stainless-steel Breville Smart Fryer that can hold a gallon of oil and costs $130, but some of them can go for lower than $30!

You won't need all of these things for every recipe, but just so there are no surprises, here's a list of some other helpful equipment, kitchen and otherwise, called for over the course of this book: kitchen stand mixer, hand mixer, blender or food processor, waffle iron, cooling rack, cookie tray or baking sheet, waffle iron, pizza stone or steel, gas or charcoal grill, sizzle platter, and tongs (always tongs).

And here are some ingredients you'll come across that you may not already have in your pantry that you may want to buy or order online in advance: Frank's RedHot Sauce, Margherita Pepperoni, celery seeds, cream of tartar, and Wondra flour.

OLD-SCHOOL BUFFALO WINGS (PAGE 23)

Iconic Buffalo Foods Timeline:
Some Important Dates in Buffalo Food History

1820s Whether you believe the Tom & Jerry was invented in the 1820s by British journalist Pierce Egan (who's said to have named the drink after characters in a popular novel) or in 1862 by Jerry Thomas, the New York City bartender who authored the first bartender guide, this once-ubiquitous drink never disappeared from Buffalo, where it's still made every winter.

1869 Joseph Sahlen founds the Sahlen Packing Company in Buffalo, dedicating the company to fresh, high-quality meat products.

1901 After living in England and Canada, Joseph A. Fowler travels to Buffalo to attend the Pan-American Exposition where he creates and sells chocolate confections and sweets. Their success leads him to open a candy store with his brother Claude.

1901 Beef on weck is thought to have originated at the Pan-American Exposition.

1901 While the term "coffee break" doesn't pop up until 1952, depending on who you believe, the coffee break originated either with Larkin Soap Company in 1901 or with Barcalo (now BarcaLounger) in 1902, with the practice of giving employees a break to drink free coffee.

1920 Jacob Frank and Adam Estilette become business partners, mixing spice, vinegar, garlic, and cayenne to create Frank's Louisiana RedHot Sauce.

1922 Heintz & Weber Co., Inc., the company that invented Weber's Brand Horseradish Mustard, is founded.

1923 Gino Silverstrini and Lee Federconi open Chef's on the corner of Seneca and Chicago.

1924 After setting up several unsuccessful doughnut shops elsewhere, Frederick Maier moves to Buffalo and opens Freddie's Doughnuts, which will go on to become one of the city's most beloved doughnut shops until it closes in 1989.

1927 Theodore "Ted" Spiro Liaros buys a tiny tool shed near the just-finished Peace Bridge to sell Ted's Hot Dogs to passersby.

1927 Santora's Pizza is born after Fioravanti Santora starts selling pizza by the slice out of his homemade ice cream shop.

1931 Bison Foods, which will go on to produce Buffalo's popular Bison sour cream dips, is founded.

1933 Angelo Costanzo starts a bakery along the Niagara River known as Costanzo's Bread. It will go on to become one of the most widely used rolls in all of Buffalo for subs.

1940s Sponge candy is said to have been invented.

1946 Louise Duffney founds Duff's as a gin mill. Duff's will start serving wings in 1969, five years after Anchor Bar.

1946 Dino Pacciotti buys a local bocce ball court and after finding an old oven in the basement, starts serving his own take on a thick, generously topped, crispy pizza with toppings edging out over the crust.

1947 Louis Russo, an immigrant from Sorrento, Italy, founds the company Sorrento Cheese, since renamed Galbani, a worldwide brand owned by Groupe Lactalis.

1957 Construction laborer and Navy vet Joe Todaro (Papa Joe) opens La Nova Pizzeria on 43 South Niagara Street in Tonawanda with his 12-year-old son Joe Jr.

1962 At Chef's (opened in 1923), former busboy-turned-owner Lou Billittier tosses spaghetti in butter and tops it with cheese that's melted and crisped under a broiler. Spaghetti Parm is born.

1964 Buffalo wings are invented by Teressa Bellissimo at the Anchor Bar.

1973 Chicago natives Andy Gerovac, Ken Koczur, Dan Scepkowski, and Bruce Robertson open the first Mighty Taco on Hertel Avenue.

1981 Jim Incorvaia opens Jim's SteakOut. Late-night eating with chicken finger and stinger subs will never be the same.

1987 Aunt Rosie's Olde Tyme Loganberry is born. Crystal Beach, the amusement park that popularized the drink (a blackberry-raspberry hybrid originated in California) with Buffalonians for decades, closes in 1989. Another popular version, PJ's Crystal Beach, is founded in 1998.

1990 A year after opening his restaurant Billy Ogden's, Andy DiVincenzo introduces his signature stuffed hot banana peppers at Taste of Buffalo.

1992 "Put down the burger, put down the dog, pick up the original Pizza Log!" Robert Cordova rolls cheese, sauce, and pepperoni in a crispy wrapper to invent the Original Pizza Logs (now Finger Food Products, Inc.), behind a grocery store in Niagara Falls.

1996 Paula Huber starts selling hand-cut homemade doughnuts made on-premises at Paula's Doughnuts.

2002 Chef Columbus "Marshall" Grady invents Bleu Bayou Wings at Abigail's in Waterloo, New York.

2008 Jim's SteakOut adds The Stinger to their menu, a sandwich said to have been invented by Colosso Taco & Subs sometime before to be determined.

OLD-SCHOOL BUFFALO WINGS (PAGE 23)

WINGS

You've heard the story before: Teressa Bellissimo invented wings for her and Frank's son and his drinking buddies late one night in Buffalo (where they're just called "wings" or "chicken wings") on the spur of the moment. Bar food was never the same again. End of story, right? Not quite.

Unbreaded and halved wings drenched with a butter-based hot sauce were said to have been first served at Anchor Bar in Buffalo by Frank and Teressa, yes, an Italian-American couple who paired them with leftover blue cheese dressing and celery from an antipasto plate at their Italian restaurant and bar. But they *may* have been inspired by the battered and fried sweet-sauce version served by a man named John Young at his restaurant. And *he* may have been inspired after hearing how well an African American-run, Chinese-owned restaurant was doing selling them in Washington, DC. And that DC sauce? It made its way to the African American community *there* from another one in Chicago.

Okay, so the story is more complicated than you may have originally heard, but the recipe is straightforward. Even though the folks at Anchor are fairly tight-lipped about their recipe, it's long been known that the key to the original wings was Frank's Louisiana RedHot Sauce. These days, it's just called Frank's RedHot, and Anchor sells a self-branded sauce, which they admit (via their label) includes cayenne, vinegar, salt, garlic, and margarine. Folks use margarine because it's cheaper. *You* won't because if you're going to go to the trouble of making wings at home, you want them to be great, and butter is better, and so is peanut oil for frying.

In fact, here's what you're going to do. You're going to trust me. Shell out the $30 bucks for a small kitchen fryer so you don't make a mess and don't have to use a thermometer. If you don't for some reason, you're going to at least use enough peanut oil to completely submerge the wings (about 10 cups or $2/_3$ of a gallon). You're also going to fry your wings for 12 minutes (and up to 16). Some instruction booklets that come with fryers say 8 to 10 minutes and they may, in fact, be right. But the best places in town these days cook them longer to make them nice and crispy. That may be because frequent use of the fryers in restaurant kitchens means they need the extra time for the oil to reach the correct temperature again. The point is, you want to serve some crispy wings. Not so cooked that they're not juicy, but crispy. And you're going to wait a minute or two between batches for the oil to climb back to the right temperature.

Celery is mandatory. Carrots are optional. Don't skimp on the napkins.

Straight from the Buffalo's Mouth (Buffalo's Wingmakers Spill)

During my research in Buffalo, I ate at dozens of the city's most heralded wing spots and interviewed many of their owners as well as the folks entrusted with making wings day in, day out. While you'll find expert advice about wings from some of the nation's most well-respected chefs in these pages, Buffalo, ground zero for wings, is obviously the place to start.

Here are a few interesting insights, tidbits, and tricks that go further than the two parts melted butter to three parts Frank's that were picked up while winging it on the Nickel City's wing trail. You'll find recipes for some in the book. Use the rest for your own wing-spiration.

ABIGAIL'S, 1978 US 20, WATERLOO, NY 13165

Abigail's was awarded the title of world's best wings in the wing documentary, *The Great Chicken Wing Hunt*. And while it's two hours east of Buffalo, it's absolutely worth it (see page 33 for the recipe). Celery and blue cheese are blended into a sauce made with Frank's RedHot Sauce to make what Chef Columbus "Marshall" Grady calls "Bleu Bayou Wings."

BAR BILL TAVERN, 185 MAIN STREET, EAST AURORA, NY 14052

Here you thought it was all about just frying and tossing with Frank's. Clark Crook, the current owner, bought Bar Bill with his wife Katie in 2011 from her Uncle Joe. Clark said that what Joe, a mechanical engineer at Bell Aircraft, did was meticulous, maniacal, and anal: "He brought engineering practices to his restaurant business," using scientific methods to retest his recipe, hone an ideal version, and then his process so that his staff could repeat it. "But his real claim to fame is that we don't shake our wings with sauce in a bowl and then dump it all onto a plate," Crook notes. "We paint each individual chicken wing with sauce on each side, so it creates an even-flavored heat profile in every bite. It makes a huge difference." I couldn't get Clark to go on the record about using real butter, but on the subject of Frank's, he was clear. "Our feeling is that if you're a Buffalo purist, then your sauce is based on Frank's," he told me. "And if it's not Frank's, it's not a Buffalo wing, in our opinion." Here's another fun thing learned at Bar Bill to employ when serving wings. "There's a little game we like to say we perfected that we call Wing Roulette, that some of our hardy fans like to participate in, where we'll disguise a Suicide (insanely spicy) wing in their order."

BASES LOADED, 3355 LAKESHORE ROAD, BLASDELL, NY 14219

These wings were a finalist in Buffalo Spree's 2015 search for the city's best (they lost out to the winner: Bar Bill Tavern). Ernie, the owner, says his wings get a 16-minute fry, and that the dressing is a premade one doctored with blue cheese. "We use Frank's, as well as a mixture of our own spices," Ernie confides.

"We try to use butter, but we use a little margarine as well." One of the most interesting wings here is a double-dipped sauce style they started doing in 2014: garlic Parm (or "stinky") wings. They're medium garlic Parmesan doused wings—spicy, funky, and cheesy—and they're not like any other you've likely tried (see page 45 for the recipe).

DOC SULLIVAN'S, 474 ABBOTT ROAD, BUFFALO, NY 14220

This South Buffalo stalwart has tavern tradition reaching back to the '30s when it was known as Smitty's. And while it has new ownership, the homemade blue cheese dressing and Smitty Wing recipe were passed on by the previous owners. The sauce is a matter of curiosity. The new owner, Tommy, says secrecy around it has led to the proliferation of "South Buffalo Style," with folks in the neighborhood trying to replicate it. The *Buffalo News* speculates it involves nutmeg, celery seed, ginger, cinnamon, and ground cloves, but Tommy denies that. What *is* Smitty Style? "A butter-based sauce with about a dozen ingredients, mixed with hot sauce, and that's it," he explained. "But the butter and seasoning make up a recipe that has to be about forty or fifty years old now."

DWYER'S, 65 WEBSTER STREET, NORTH TONAWANDA, NY 14120

There are two versions of Frank's-based wing sauces at Dwyer's: Buffalo style and Dwyer's style. In addition to a few secret ingredients that owner Greg Stenis wouldn't share, the key difference is the addition of vinegar to the Dwyer's style. Greg did say that he orders wings from his bar under an anonymous name once or twice a week to test out their quality and that he uses a butter substitute instead of the real thing, noting that he doesn't think most people can tell the difference. Nobody, he says, has ever asked. But he is a Frank's man. "I haven't found one yet that's dead-on for Frank's," he told me. "People come in all the time and try to sell me on their sauce, but nothing comes close. It just has the right balance of not being too hot and having lots of flavor."

ELMO'S, 2349 MILLERSPORT HIGHWAY, GETZVILLE, NY 14068

This is one of Buffalo's wing joints that has embraced, and even suggests that you "Double Dip," mixing wings in two different sauces to create new flavors, like Cajun Barbecue and Cajun hot! The processes that go into the Cajun wings and double-dipped Cajun-Barbecue wings are a little mind-bending. They're actually a fried-grilled affair (wings are pulled out of the fryer early to compensate). Elmo's Cajun wings are fried, tossed in a vinegar and reinforced Frank's RedHot sauce (with black pepper, mustard, garlic, cayenne, and horseradish), and then grilled. Their *double-dipped* wings are fried, sauced, grilled, then sauced. And their Cajun-barbecue wings are fried, shaken in Cajun sauce, grilled to blacken them, then tossed in honey or barbecue sauce. If you're confused, take this away: Doubling up on cooking techniques is something you see in classic French cuisine. Think of that roast you've pan-seared and then roasted. Grilling fried wings adds dimensions: bitterness, caramelization, crunch, and crispiness. If your head is spinning, consider the off-menu triple-dipped wings! They go in the fryer, get done Cajun-style (are doused in a barbecue sauce that includes hot honey mustard and Cajun seasoning and grilled), grilled *barbecue*, and *then* covered with a final coating of a homemade extra hot sauce.

GENE McCARTHY'S, 73 HAMBURG STREET, BUFFALO, NY 14204

When current owner Bill Roenigk took over, Gene McCarthy's did hot, medium, and mild. These days, Gene McCarthy's doesn't use Frank's, instead employing a sweet and spicy barbecue sauce. They've also since invented two signature wing styles. The Sheffield employs a dry rub with oregano and Cajun spices (along with a few other secret ingredients). The other is a pairing you don't frequently see: tiny crumbles of blue cheese are folded into barbecue sauce and tossed with the wings and scattered on top. "That was one of our inventions," Bill explained. "We named it after Gene." Mixing blue cheese's umami funk into wing sauces is an underemployed move and you have to wonder why. It's a serious flavor enhancer that solves the problem of trying to adhere blue cheese dressing to a wing already slick with sauce.

JUDI'S, 2057 MILITARY ROAD, NIAGARA FALLS, NY 14304

The salt-and-pepper application is something you typically see applied to shrimp and pork chops in Chinatown. At Judi's, which says they only use trans-fat-free oil, it means that if you're a crisp fanatic, you've found your happy place. It's all chicken flavor and crunchy skin on wings not soggied with sauce, wings that haven't spent even a minute out of the fryer before you get them. It's a preparation you wish you'd see more often. Same with the Cajun dry seasoning, which can also be applied with hot sauce, a tactic where wings are coated with Cajun spice and then sauce-tossed. The result is a peppery blast to the tongue that's a bit like licking a five-o'clock shadow.

KELLY'S KORNER, 2526 DELAWARE AVENUE, BUFFALO, NY 14216

As soon as the wings are set down, you notice the homemade touch. There's no Frank's red sheen—instead, you see flecks of red pepper seeds in a sauce that clings to the cracks, crevices, and corners of every fried surface and pools in a small puddle of one or two tablespoons under the wings on the plate. There's a pale beige fry on the sides of the wings with crispy ends and a pleasant, cayenne burn with little to no vinegary tang.

LOVEJOY, 900 MAIN STREET, BUFFALO, NY 14202

If there's a case to be made for wings made using liquid butter, co-owner Anthony Kulik is making it at his Lovejoy pizzeria. Truth be told, Kulik doesn't make his sauce with the liquid stuff full-on but says he cuts the real thing with the liquid to help offset the cost of butter. You'd be hard-pressed to tell his superior wings from a sauce made with straight butter. Asked for the secrets to bat-and-flat greatness, Kulik says, "You need a fresh-cut wing, a wing that's big, but not too big," Kulik tells me. "You shouldn't have to take more than three bites of a wing. The thing should be done within two to three bites." Like a few other places around town, he also does a Cajun-style wing, which (also like other Buffalo spots) he claims is the greatest wing in the whole city.

MAMMOSER'S, 16 SOUTH BUFFALO STREET, HAMBURG, NY 14075

Owner Peter Dimfle says their sauce has its origins with his mother in the '70s. They had a big garden. His mother was into spicy foods, and one day she just sat down and started mixing up some stuff for a wing sauce. It's a cayenne-based sauce, which Dimfle claims makes the heat stick to the wings better, and they don't use butter or margarine. In the early years, he says they were mixing it with a drill motor in five-gallon buckets, but since 1978, they've been getting the recipe bottled.

NINE-ELEVEN TAVERN, 11 BLOOMFIELD AVENUE, BUFFALO, NY 14220

"I make all my sauce hot, alright?" owner and cook Mark Gress says matter-of-factly. "So if you buy a jar of sauce here, you're not going to get medium or mild, you're just going to get hot, and I'll tell you how to cut that to make it medium or mild." The key to that? Using clarified butter to make his sauce, which you don't hear of most wing makers doing, and which Gress says he also does for flavor.

WIECHEC'S, 1748 CLINTON STREET, KAISERTOWN, NY 14206

Wiechec's is famous for their Friday fish fry. And that Catholic tradition has a direct effect on the menu because the fryers are otherwise occupied with fish. Devotees know that, as the menu notes, chicken wings are *not available Fridays between 11 AM and 9 PM*. When wings are on the offer, they come with Ken's blue cheese dressing and big, thick sticks of celery. They're also another practitioner of the medium garlic Parmesan wings, which Bases Loaded calls "Stinky" but are called "Red Sox" wings here.

SO YOU'RE MAKING BUFFALO SAUCE— HOW VERY . . . FRENCH OF YOU

That's right—believe it or not, Buffalo sauce isn't far from being *beurre blanc*, a fancy French sauce made with reduced vinegar and shallots. After all, the primary ingredient of hot sauce is vinegar, and wing sauce is just a combination of melted butter and hot sauce. There are even wing sauce recipes that call for shallots and garlic. It's just flipped on its head: Beurre blanc is a vinegar that's been reduced, then had butter added to it; and Buffalo sauce is melted butter that you add a vinegary hot sauce to. Anyway, it's ridiculously easy to make, and you can put it on most everything (thus Frank's "I put that @$%& on everything" campaign).

Where did Frank's come from? How did it end up being *the* preferred hot sauce for wings? The story begins with Jacob Frank, who founded the Frank Tea and Spice Company in 1896, in Cincinnati, Ohio. Frank partnered with pepper farmer Adam Estilette in New Iberia, Louisiana, in 1918 to create a cayenne pepper-spiced sauce, and the first bottle of Frank's RedHot Sauce was bottled in 1920. The ingredients are simple and few—aged cayenne red peppers, distilled vinegar, water, salt, and garlic powder—but paired with butter to create magic. As for how it ended up being used by Teressa Bel-

lissimo at Anchor Bar in Buffalo, one report has it that she picked it off the shelf at the supermarket because it had the same name as her husband.

The original recipe was once subject to great speculation, and, while Anchor makes and bottles their own sauce these days (they're reported to use a butter substitute), Frank's recommends tossing wings in two parts melted butter to three parts Frank's. This recipe adds an additional vinegary touch known to have been used by wing-slingers over the years. If you're a little heat-shy, add more butter for a milder sauce. If you're a heat freak, go heavier on the hot sauce and reduce the amount of butter. Whatever you do, I'd recommend about one batch of sauce to every 12 to 18 wings. That may leave you with extra, but there's no bigger pain than watching fresh wings die while you rummage around to make more sauce.

Remember, this recipe is just a base. Places in Buffalo trick out their sauces, adding spices, hot peppers, honey, sriracha, bourbon, you name it. Make a batch of the original so you know what you're doing, and then add whatever other ingredients you think will make for awesome wings.

BUFFALO WING SAUCE

PREP TIME: 3 minutes ★ **COOKING TIME:** 3 minutes ★ **YIELD:** Slightly less than 1 cup

⅓ cup butter, melted
½ cup Frank's RedHot Sauce
1 tablespoon white vinegar (optional)

1. Melt butter in a saucepan over medium-low heat. Don't brown it!

2. Add hot sauce and optional vinegar. Whisk until well combined.

BUFFALO WINGS

How do you make great wings?

Alton Brown says to steam them for 10 minutes, dry them, refrigerate them for an hour, then bake them in a 425°F oven for 40 to 50 minutes, turning them once (he also says you only need ¼ cup of sauce for a dozen wings, which is insanely sparse). Food Network recommends 375°F for 15 minutes (they advise 1½ cups of sauce to 36 wings). *Serious Eats* wants you to double-fry confit by first cooking them in oil from room temperature to 250°F for 20 minutes, resting them for an hour or covering and resting them in the fridge for three nights, then frying them at 400°F for 10 minutes (1 cup of sauce per 48 wings). *Bon Appétit* wants you to dredge them in cornstarch, fry them at 375°F for 10 to 12 minutes, then keep them warm in the oven while you fry up other batches. *Food & Wine* advises you to bake them for 45 minutes in a 500°F oven. Frank's says to bake them at 450°F for a half hour, turning once (at least they recommend nearly a cup of sauce per dozen wings). And in the *New York Times*, Mark Bittman says to grill them for 15 to 20 minutes (and stretch less than ⅔ of a cup of sauce over 36 wings).

I belabor this for context, to show how varied and complicated wing recipes are. I tell you because, fellow wingnut, I love you. You're *welcome* to try all of these techniques. But if you've eaten at dozens of wing joints in Buffalo like I have, you know baked wings will never be as good as fried ones (and that they take longer to make too). And if you've talked with the owners and cooks at the Nickel City's most vaunted establishments, you know that any place that promises wings in 15 minutes or less *from the time you order them* is serving wings that aren't fresh. Most likely, they've par-cooked wings that are sitting in a fry basket above the oil. Most of Buffalo's best wing-makers say wings should be fried between 350°F to 375°F for anywhere between 12 to 20 minutes and typically no less than 15 to 16. And that's *just to cook fresh wings to the right crispiness*.

Keep this in mind when you're making wings at home: you're going to want to submerge them in oil already brought up to the desired temperature for at least 15 minutes. And don't skimp on the sauce. Have you seen a legit plate of wings in Buffalo? Then you've seen the heavy sauce slick left on the plate. Plan on about ⅔ of a cup per 18 wings.

OLD-SCHOOL BUFFALO WINGS

PREP TIME: 20 minutes ★ **COOKING TIME:** 48 minutes to 1 hour and 4 minutes ★
SERVES: 4 people ★ **YIELD:** 24 wings

1 cup Homemade Blue Cheese Dressing (page 38)

2 celery stalks, sliced into sticks

2 carrots, peeled and sliced into sticks, or 24 baby carrots (6 per wing batch)

2 dozen chicken wings cut into flats and drumettes (about 2 pounds)

continued

Kosher salt

Freshly ground black pepper

Enough peanut oil to submerge wings (8 to 10 cups)

2 cups Buffalo Wing Sauce (page 22), warmed

1. Prepare Blue Cheese Dressing, celery, and carrot sticks.

2. If not already done, cut off wingtips, and cut wing and drumstick at the joint. Dry wings thoroughly. Season wings with salt and pepper.

3. Heat oil until it reaches 350 to 355°F. As the oil warms, prepare Buffalo Wing Sauce.

4. In batches of six, cook wings 16 minutes, gently lowering them into the oil and jostling the basket occasionally (or poking with a dry wooden spoon). Check the wings at the 12-minute mark. When wings are golden brown, drain, remove, and dry 1 minute on a tray lined with paper towels.

5. Wait a moment for the oil to regain temperature. Toss the batch of fried wings into a large bowl, drizzle ½ cup sauce over them, and toss in the bowl until completely covered. Serve on a large, warm plate and pour some of the remaining sauce used to coat them in the bowl to cover. Serve with Blue Cheese Dressing, and celery and carrot sticks.

6. Repeat process, frying, drying, and saucing until remaining batches are cooked.

Great Chefs, Great Wings: Dale Talde on Wings

Chef Dale Talde isn't from Buffalo, but a few years ago, his wings were singled out by *Food & Wine* magazine as among America's best. He burst onto the national culinary scene via two seasons of Bravo's *Top Chef*, when his frank, no-BS personality made him one of the more entertaining chefs in the show's history. But this CIA-trained cook is more than a TV chef. He's worked for the likes of Jean Georges (he helped open Vong in Chicago) and Masaharu Morimoto (whom he helped open Morimoto in New York City). With his unique blend of Asian and American cuisines (he once said he's "trying to take the dirty word out of fusion"), this Chicago native and son of Filipino immigrants makes some of the boldest, most creative food in the country—think stoner food on methamphetamines.

Dishes like pretzel pork and chive dumplings with spicy mustard, Korean fried chicken with crispy oyster-bacon pad Thai, and, of course, kung pao chicken wings have made Chef Talde's eponymous Brooklyn restaurant Talde, which he owns with partners David Massoni and John Bush, one of Park Slope's most popular spots.

To make the dump-and-stir sauce for these wings, Talde makes a Szechuan oil that he mixes with toban djan, oyster sauce, wine, vinegar, chili sauce, and sesame oil. He coats them in a rice flour batter, then fries them until they're lightly golden. They get garnished with peanuts, cilantro, and scallions. They're buzzy, spicy, and insanely good.

I caught up with Chef Talde to get his wing philosophy and to ask about the noise around the online conversation about air-chilling, double-frying, and par-cooking them overnight before serving.

Your kung pao wings have been named some of the best in America. How'd they come about?

Chef Dale Talde: I always had the sauce in my back pocket. I was at another restaurant and we were running it with a fish dish. We were cooking the fish, then covering it in kung pao sauce, and it was delicious. We ran the dish but they had made so much sauce, and were like, "Hey what do you want us to do with this sauce?" And I said, "Well, you got a lot of wings," cause it's the weekend. So we do wings on Saturdays, and Sundays for brunch. And I was like, if you have a lot of wings left over, and you have a lot of extra sauce, do a wing special and do it at the bar for Monday Night Football.

So it started as a special.

Two guys came in and ordered two orders each, back-to-back, and they were like, "Those were great. Could we get another?" And then they just started coming. Every table had an order and the same group of guys came back a week after and were like, "Hey, we want those wings."

"Sorry we don't have them."

"Oh my god, you got to put them on the menu."

Then it was like, alright, and we just ran with it.

Buttermilk wouldn't be the first thing you'd think to pair with kung pao. How'd that come about?

You need something to cool it down, it's just so spicy. The kung pao wings are fairly aggressively seasoned, salty, sweet, sour—you need some relief.

Your recipe for the sauce calls for Shaoxing wine. What if you can't find that?

Try sherry.

You guys double-fry your wings once at 275°F, then again at 325°F. What's your philosophy on double-frying?

It's more of a restaurant thing. We're not cooking wings to order in 15 minutes. You want to just cook them through, and then the second time, fry them to get them hot. You cook them low to cook them through softly and the second time you cook them hard to crisp them.

You've been known to also make your wings using rice flour. Why?

It's just a light coating so it gives the sauce something to stick to. I like the texture and I like how crispy it gets. It's a gluten-free substitute. So the kung pao wings are more heavily breaded than the other ones, the ones that are just dredged in rice flour and fried, but they're still cooked twice. And our Buffalo sauce is our take. It's Frank's RedHot, sriracha, honey, butter, and garlic.

What are your thoughts on cooking and overnight cooling?

If you're gonna cook them at home just cook it all the way through once. And then toss and serve.

There are those who will say that you should par-cook them and cool them in the fridge overnight to increase the crispiness.

What's going to be better than cooking them fresh? Just cook it fresh. Don't waste your time on that. It's just an extra step. Simple is always better.

What are your thoughts on baked wings?

If you suck you can do a baked version. Like look in the mirror and ask, "Do I suck?" And if you suck a little bit then put them in the oven a little bit. If you're like, "Okay, I kind of suck," then say okay, put them in the oven for a little bit less. That's a more introspective approach to wings. You got to be a little bit introspective for that.

Oil?

Regular vegetable oil. Something that can take some abuse. Peanut oil can take some abuse. Any oil that can take a little abuse. Peanut oil is best.

What's your philosophy on making great wings?

Just fat, acid, heat, and salt. That's it. Those are the essentials any wing recipe has to include. Even if we're talking about some sweet honey barbecue wings, they still need acid, they still need fat, they still need barbecue spice. That's my philosophy.

BAKED BUFFALO WINGS (A.K.A. THE MORE INTROSPECTIVE APPROACH TO WINGS)

Nobody, I mean nobody, who is serious about their chicken wings bakes them. Okay, strike that. Nearly nobody (save Chef Columbus "Marshal" Grady in Waterloo, NY; page 32), who is serious about their wings bakes them. *Certainly* not in Buffalo's bars and restaurants.

"The thing that really is bad about chicken wings is that they started to bake them," chided the *Buffalo News*'s former restaurant critic Janice Okun, referring to the proliferation of recipes for making wings at home. "Why do they bake them? They bake them because they think they are healthy. Don't tell me about baked chicken wings. I think they're awful."

Wow. Between Janice and Dale Talde, wing bakers face some stern condemnation. And it's hard to argue with the crisp factor of fried wings. But . . . but, but, but . . . if you *are* going to bake your wings, whether it's because you don't want to (or can't) make kitchen counter space commitment to a small, cheap fryer or you don't have the energy to clean up the mess that frying in a pot *does* inevitably visit to your stovetop, there *is* a secret way to give baked wings a crisp factor that's pretty close to the blistered skin you get from frying. And it's called baking powder.

The idea goes something like this. Tossing wings in baking powder will raise their pH (if you recall the biology lesson, the "potential of hydrogen" is a measure of acidity or alkalinity), making them more alkaline. That leaves you with fewer hydrogen ions and more hydroxide ions, making the skin more susceptible to browning. That, plus air-drying your wings in the fridge to wick out their moisture, will add surface area to the skin and lead to juicy, crispier wings closer to (some will argue indiscernible from) what you'd get from the fryer.

Here's the rub: we're talking about air-drying wings in your fridge from 8 to 24 hours. So either prep wings *a day* in advance, keep them out raw in your fridge for a day, *then* bake them for an hour, or fry them for 16 to 18 minutes and (if you don't have a fryer) clean your stovetop.

BAKED BUFFALO WINGS

PREP TIME: 8 hours and 15 minutes to 24 hours and 15 minutes ★

COOKING TIME: 50 minutes ★ **YIELD:** 24 wings

2 dozen chicken wings cut into flats and drumettes (about 2 pounds)

1 tablespoon baking powder (1½ teaspoons per pound)

2 teaspoons kosher salt (1 teaspoon per pound)

2 cups Buffalo Wing Sauce (page 22), warmed

1 cup Homemade Blue Cheese Dressing (page 38)

2 celery stalks, sliced into sticks

2 carrots, peeled and sliced into sticks, or 24 baby carrots (6 per wing batch)

1. If not already done, cut off wingtips, and cut wing and drumstick at the joint.

2. Using paper towels, meticulously dry every wing to remove all moisture.

3. Line a baking sheet with foil and set a baking/cooling rack on top.

4. Thoroughly toss wings in baking powder and salt, then layer them on the rack, leaving enough space for a wing between each. Place in fridge and air dry uncovered for 24 hours (8 at a minimum).

continued

5. Arrange oven rack in the high position, then preheat oven to 450°F.

6. Put wings on the high rack and bake 20 minutes.

7. Prep Buffalo Wing Sauce, Blue Cheese Dressing, celery, and carrots.

8. Flip wings and bake 15 minutes. Flip again and bake 15 more minutes.

9. Toss in Buffalo Wing Sauce, serve on a large, warm plate, and pour some of the remaining sauce over the wings. Serve with Blue Cheese Dressing, celery, and carrots.

Great Chefs, Great Wings: José Andrés on Wings

José Andrés is one of the world's great chefs. Among his 30-some restaurants are The Bazaar in Los Angeles and Miami, one of America's most creative restaurants, and an even more innovative spot, minibar in Washington DC. While this über-chef's background is in Spanish and modernist cuisines, he's also known for having masterfully taken on Mexican, Peruvian, Chinese, and Middle Eastern cooking. He's been named one of *TIME* magazine's 100 Most Influential People in World, and is working with the Adrià brothers of El Bulli fame on a Spanish food hall in New York City's Hudson Yards development. Blink and you're bound to miss something delicious that the chef has done.

No surprise, then, that his take on Buffalo wings at The Bazaar has been singled out by *Food & Wine* as among some of *the best* in the country. They are listed as "Boneless Mary's Farm Buffalo Chicken Wings with cheese and celery." Five of these beautiful bite-size wings come per order, their crackly skin shiny with sauce, topped with a tiny chopped celery cubes, a ridge of blue cheese dressing, and a celery sprig. They're outrageous.

What kind of chicken do you prefer to source for wings?

Chef José Andrés: Wings from Mary's Free Range Chickens raised in the San Joaquin Valley in California.

To double-fry or not?

We do not double-fry. We confit* the wings for eight minutes and then debone them before frying. We dust them in a flour and Trisol mixture (Trisol is a wheat-derived fiber designed for crisp batters—you could substitute rice flour), and then shallow fry in a pan. We use a blended oil: 25 percent olive oil and 75 percent canola oil.

What's the optimum cooking time?

Well, we marinate them for 12 hours before we cook them. After confit-ing the wings, we only fry them a few minutes on each side. I don't go on time but on look—when the wings are golden-brown and crispy.

Where does the heat come from on your wings?

We use "José's hot sauce," which is cayenne and sherry-vinegar-based, and add it to a chicken demi-glace**for the sauce that coats the wings. For our sides, we brunoise*** celery and compress it in celery juice, and make our own blue cheese sauce, using blue cheese from Shaft's in Cedar Ridge, California.

* In French, *confit* means "to preserve." A food that has been confited has been cooked slowly in grease, oil, or syrup, at a low temperature over a long period of time as a method of preservation.

** A demi-glace is a rich brown stock reduction used in classic French cuisine.

*** Brunoise is a knife cut involving matchstick slices that are then cut to form cubes about one to three milimeters squared.

WHY DIDN'T *WE* THINK OF THAT?!
CHEF MARSHAL GRADY'S BLEU BAYOU WINGS

Director Matt Reynolds hit more than 70 wing spots (!) in New York State on an epic adventure to seek out the best wings for his film, *The Great Chicken Wing Hunt*. He settled on the Bleu Bayou Wings at Abigail's, a restaurant that is two hours east of Buffalo in the town of Waterloo, where wings' traditional condiments—celery, Frank's RedHot, and blue cheese—are incorporated *into* the hot sauce that coats them.

The inspiration for Bleu Bayou Wings glistens with a brilliance that smacks of Teressa Bellissimo's eureka moment. But it was all about building a better mousetrap. "I was just thinking, there's

gotta be a better way to do this because of the condiments," their inventor, Chef Columbus "Marshal" Grady told me. "People like to dip, but if you were to mix everything together, you'd get all the flavors and not have to worry about dipping in the blue cheese because it would just be in the sauce. You don't have to worry about the celery because it's in the sauce."

Modest fame followed, including a write-up in *The Wall Street Journal*, but Grady didn't rush to share his award-winning recipe. When I visited, I discovered you can buy the bottled sauce (mild and hot), and that Grady was still fairly mum . . . at first.

"Celery and blue cheese and the Frank's RedHot Sauce, that's as far as I go," he said when I pried.

But he *did* share some details. He said he uses at least 60 ounces of Frank's RedHot per gallon and that the sauce doesn't get cooked (it goes right on). He also said that Sysco blue cheese is the house blue dressing, and that two ounces of sauce goes on each order (a dozen wings). Perhaps most interesting is that Grady uses a cooking technique unemployed by most wingmakers, going against the canon. "I bake my wings for 35 to 45 minutes at 350°F, then I fry 'em another seven to eight minutes until they're crispy at 325°F," he said, adding that he seasons them with salt and pepper first.

Some of that math might be kitchen-hazed. While eating an order, I estimated that there were likely three tablespoons of sauce on each wing and about another half a cup of sauce *under* the wings on the plate. (And they were somehow still crispy!) But all these details, along with the experience of tasting a celery-flecked sauce as thick as a cheese soup, are cardinal points that, with a little experimentation, lead to a recipe that, if not exact, closely approximates Grady's chicken wings. This recipe mimics Chef Grady's baked-fried technique, but I'd encourage you to just make the sauce and use it on wings you fry up the same way you cook them using the old-school recipe (page 23). The recipe's going to make extra, even after going for that extra saucy Abigail's effect, so you'll have some to try on fish, steak, and what have you. Either way, while digging into this or the original, prepare yourself for *at least* a six-napkin experience.

═══ CHEF MARSHAL GRADY'S BLEU BAYOU WINGS ═══

PREP TIME: 20 to 30 minutes ★ **COOKING TIME:** 55 minutes ★

YIELD: 3½ cups sauce and 24 wings

2 dozen chicken wings cut into flats and drumettes (about 2 pounds)

Kosher salt

Freshly ground black pepper

1½ cups Homemade Blue Cheese Dressing (page 38), with ½ cup reserved for the Bleu Bayou Sauce

7 celery stalks, 2 sliced into sticks (for garnish), 5 peeled and finely minced (about 1 cup)

1 cup butter

6 cloves garlic, minced

3 Thai chiles

1 cup Frank's RedHot Sauce

1 tablespoon sriracha

½ teaspoon cayenne pepper

1 teaspoon garlic powder

1 teaspoon onion powder

2 tablespoons white vinegar

½ cup crumbled blue cheese

1. If you're going to make the wings à la Chef Grady, preheat oven to 350°F. If you're just going to make the sauce, start at step 4.

2. If not already done, cut off wingtips, and cut wing and drumstick at the joint. Dry wings thoroughly. Season wings with salt and pepper. Bake for 35 to 45 minutes.

continued

3. Preheat fryer (or pot of vegetable oil) to 325°F.

4. Prepare Blue Cheese Dressing and celery (just the minced if you're only making the sauce).

5. In a saucepan over medium heat, melt butter without burning or coloring it.

6. Add garlic and chiles and cook 2 to 3 minutes.

7. Whisk in Frank's, sriracha, cayenne, garlic and onion powders, and vinegar until well combined. Simmer on low for 5 minutes then remove from heat to a large bowl.

8. Add ½ cup Blue Cheese Dressing and minced celery into wing sauce and thoroughly combine. (The Bleu Bayou Sauce is done at this point.)

9. Transfer baked wings from oven to fryer. Fry 7 to 8 minutes, toss in Bleu Bayou Sauce, plate, then drizzle another ½ cup of sauce over the wings and serve with a side of Blue Cheese Dressing and celery.

Great Chefs, Great Wings: Andy Ricker on His Favorite Wing-Frying Oil

The wings at James Beard award–winning Chef Andy Ricker's famed Portland restaurant Pok Pok are so good, they've gained a following at his Brooklyn location and been the star on their own with spinoff, Pok Pok Wing. Ricker, who credits the recipe to his daytime cook Ike on his menu (they're called Ike's Vietnamese Fish Sauce Wings) has gone so far as to call them Pok Pok's signature dish.

To make the wings, Ricker presses garlic with salt, then mixes it with water and strains the liquid to marinate the wings with sugar and fish sauce (the straining allows him to get that garlic flavor without getting burnt garlic when he fries the wings). Then he tosses his uncut wings in "wing dust," a rice flour and tempura mixture, and fries them. Phu Quoc fish sauce and sugar gets reduced in a pan on the stovetop with chili paste; the wings get tossed in that glaze, topped with some fried garlic; and then make someone very happy.

I caught up with Chef Ricker for some quick insight into what goes into making his great wings.

What kind of chicken do you prefer to source for wings?

Andy Ricker: We use a natural product from Draper Valley Farms, which is based in Washington and Oregon.

To double-fry or not?

Yes, double-fry.

Any details you can share about how you make your signature wings?

We use fish sauce as the key seasoning and flavoring agent in our wings.

What's the optimum cooking time for great wings?

That depends on temperature, the size of wings, the type of oil used, the type of vessel used to fry in, whether you bread, batter, dredge, or put nothing on the wing.

What kinds of oil are best for wings?

We use either rice bran oil or a non-trans fat fryer oil. But the best oil to use, in my opinion, is palm oil because it is a saturated fat. Sorry, but saturated fat oils work best for frying.

LAISSEZ LES BON TEMPS ROULER

Elmo's is next to a little Vietnamese restaurant in a strip mall on Millersport Highway (263) on the outskirts of the city in a hamlet called Getzville. It's a 20-minute drive northeast of downtown and it's worth the trip. The processes that go into the Cajun wings and double-dipped Cajun-Barbecue wings are a little mind-bending. The bar's Cajun wings go back to the early '90s, when then-cook Adam Blake was messing around and trying to create a "blackened" wing. They're actually a *fried-grilled* affair.

If you're confused, take this away: Doubling up on cooking techniques is something you see in classic French cuisine. Think of that roast you've sautéed and then roasted. Or that pan-seared duck thrown into the oven. Grilling wings that have already been fried adds extra flavor dimensions: bitterness, caramelization, crunch, crispiness. And while fried-grilled wings, known in Buffalo as pit-roasted wings (page 43), are a way of life in town—usually tossed in barbecue sauce—Elmo's adds a flavor dimension not frequently experienced. Their

Cajun wings (invented in 1993) are first fried, then tossed in vinegar and Frank's RedHot reinforced with secret ingredients, and *then* those are grilled.

Then there are their Cajun-Barbecue wings, which came about when someone who'd ordered barbecued wings got an order of Cajun instead. The mistake wings were shook up in barbecue sauce, returned to the customer, and went off the charts. The process for making them evolved a bit, and it's best to leave their description to their inventor, Adam Blake: "You throw the wings in the fryer, get them crispy, shake them in Cajun sauce, grill them to make them blackened, then you take them off the grill, literally from the grill, with two spatulas, lift up the wings, put them in the honey, or put in the barbecue sauce in a bowl, shake them and plate them."

Adam was kind enough to share some of the ingredients in the Cajun-barbecue wings, but his ingredient ratios were out of bounds. Here's my interpretation of their gobsmacking good wings.

ELMO'S CAJUN–BARBECUE WINGS

PREP TIME: 30 minutes ★ **COOKING TIME:** 1 hour ★

YIELD: 2 cups Cajun-barbecue sauce and 24 wings

⅔ cup butter

2 teaspoons fresh garlic, pressed

1 cup Frank's RedHot Sauce

2 tablespoons white vinegar

1 teaspoon kosher salt

1 teaspoon freshly ground black
   pepper

1 teaspoon mustard powder

1 teaspoon garlic powder

2 teaspoons horseradish

2 dozen chicken wings cut into flats and
   drumettes (about 2 pounds)

1 cup of your favorite store-bought or
   homemade barbecue sauce

1. Melt butter in a saucepan over medium-low heat. Add fresh garlic and cook 2 minutes.

2. Add hot sauce, vinegar, pepper, mustard, garlic powder, and horseradish to create the Cajun sauce. Whisk until well combined. Remove from heat to a large bowl.

3. Preheat fryer (or a pot with enough oil to cover) to 350°F.

4. If not already done, cut off wingtips, and cut wing and drumstick at the joint. Dry wings thoroughly. Season wings with salt and pepper.

5. Preheat grill.

6. Fry 6 wings 10 to 12 minutes. Drain, toss in a bowl lined with paper towels, then toss in the bowl of Cajun sauce.

7. Place wings on the grill with ample space between them. Cook 3 minutes then flip wings. Cook 3 more minutes, then remove to a bowl filled with barbecue sauce. Toss and serve.

BLUE CHEESE DRESSING NOT HOMEMADE? YOU BLEU IT

So here's something that may (or may not) surprise you about the blue cheese dressing you get with wings in Buffalo: it's not likely to be homemade. Many places even serve wings with a small, foil-sealed container of blue cheese dressing. And even if it's not coming from an individually packaged, commercially branded container, you may just as likely be getting brand stuff portioned out from larger containers from Sysco. Many places in Buffalo, probably 85 percent or higher, don't make their own. And you can argue that there's nothing wrong with that. "You're already eating something that's not exactly healthy," the argument goes, "what's a little soybean oil and corn syrup?"

There's a time and a place for store-bought stuff (guests at the door, nearing the end of a wing party, and you're running out of the stuff you made, etc.). Some restaurateurs even claim that folks complain if wings arrive with anything but a container of "Buffalo Bleu Cheese" with its iconic blue-rim and signature Ken's Steak House logo. And that's unequivocally better than dipping your wings in ranch dressing (what kind of animal are you!?). Local Buffalo food writer Christa Glennie Seychew put it bluntly: "Sysco blue cheese sauce NO. Ken's is acceptable."

The key to blue cheese dressing being great is twofold. You don't want a dressing that's too thin (or too thick) or you won't get proper adherence of creamy, soothing dressing to crispy wing that's already drenched in hot sauce. Second, ideally, the dressing will have blue cheese nuggets throughout. A thin dressing without any blue cheese niblets? Unless you're trying for something that pours a little better for a salad.

Blue cheese dressing serves several purposes, besides being delicious. Not only does it provide

contrast and relief from the spiciness of the wing sauce, but for the impatient, it can also temper the temperature of wings hot out of the fryer. For another variation on the recipe below, depending on the consistency you like, try blending all of the ingredients and adding another ¼ cup of crumbled cheese to the final dressing for a well-balanced funk throughout.

= HOMEMADE BLUE CHEESE DRESSING (FOR WINGS) =

PREP TIME: 10 minutes ★ **YIELD:** 2½ cups

⅓ cup mayonnaise (for homemade, page 100)

⅓ cup sour cream

⅓ cup buttermilk dressing

3 teaspoons lemon juice

2 teaspoons white vinegar

1 clove garlic, pressed

1 teaspoon onion, pressed

4 ounces soft Gorgonzola (or your favorite blue cheese), crumbled

2 tablespoons minced chives (optional)

Kosher salt

Pinch of white pepper

1. Combine all ingredients in a mixing bowl (or food processor), reserving half the blue cheese. Mix until thoroughly combined.

2. Crumble in the remaining blue cheese in small nuggets. Stir well. Chill for 1 hour if possible.

MAKING FRANK'S, ER . . . (YOUR NAME HERE)'S HOMEMADE HOT SAUCE

Along with butter, Frank's RedHot Sauce is the key ingredient every red-blooded American food obsessive knows is used to make Buffalo wings' sauce. The sauce precedes its most famous food pairing by about 44 years. Jacob Frank founded the Frank Tea and Spice Company in 1896 near the banks of the Ohio River in Cincinnati, Ohio. In 1918, Frank partnered with pepper farmer Adam Estilette in New Iberia, Louisiana, to create a cayenne pepper–spiced sauce. The first bottle of Frank's RedHot Sauce emerged from Estilette's pickling plant in 1920.

And while there's certainly no shame in using Frank's (many will say they're not *really* chicken wings without it), if you really want to wing-geek out, make your own version from scratch. After all, per the label, the ingredients in Frank's original sauce are simple and few: aged cayenne red peppers, distilled vinegar, water, salt, and garlic powder. Frank's ferments their peppers and they keep their recipe close to the vest, but you can make your own version that's really pretty easy by fermenting the peppers in a jar for even just three days.

There's little to fear: Fermentation is one of mankind's oldest methods of preserving food. You're basically creating an anaerobic (that's without oxygen, remember) environment (the brine) for lactic acid bacteria to break down the peppers' carbohydrates into acid. The acid, in turn, does the preserving. The whole process makes the ingredients more digestible and the flavors more nuanced. Just remember: Smells rotten, throw it out, sour's what it's all about.

I turned to a former colleague, Craig Kanarick, cofounder of the Internet firm Razorfish and founder of indie food site Mouth.com as my lacto-fermentation hot sauce guru. He got into lacto-fermentation years ago because he wanted to be healthier, but after a while he found it was also just cheaper to *make* things like this. He's also the only person I know who has had a 25-year obsession with *one* hot sauce (one-time Boston chef Chris Schlesinger's, which disappeared for decades before reappearing as Inner Beauty Hot Sauce—it *is* obsession-worthy) so I knew I could trust him on this.

Hey, you never know, monkeying around by substituting or adding in other peppers or ingredients could lead to the next leap forward in wing flavor technology.

HOMEMADE HOT SAUCE

PREP TIME: 3 days to 2 years (3 days minimum), and 10 minutes (10 minutes active) ★

COOKING TIME: 25 minutes ★ **YIELD:** 3 to 4 cups

3 cups bottled spring water

½ tablespoon sea salt (non-iodized)

20 fresh cayenne peppers, destemmed and
   sliced (or blend)

4 cloves garlic, minced

½ onion, minced

2 cabbage leaves

1 cup distilled white vinegar

1. To make the brine, warm water over medium heat until it starts to bubble. Add salt, stir to dissolve, then allow water to reach room temperature.

2. Don't wash the peppers. Instead, slice (or blend) them and add with garlic and onion in a large mason jar.

3. When the brine cools, pour it over the vegetables in the jar.

4. Top with two cabbage leaves to keep the peppers submerged. There should be at least an inch or so from the top of the liquid to the lip of the jar.

5. Place a plate on top of the jar and top it with something to weight the plate down.

6. Set on a counter in a cool place away from direct sunlight for anywhere from 3 days, 3 months, or 2 years (your choice depending on your level of commitment and what kind of flavor you're trying to develop!), stirring once daily to prevent mold.

7. After 3 days, the brine should become cloudy and smell a little sour. If you're ready to make your sauce, place the bottle you're planning to use to store it in a large pot with enough water to cover. Bring water to a boil over high heat and boil 5 minutes. Remove bottle using tongs, drain, and let cool.

8. Remove cabbage leaves. Pour mixture into a blender, add vinegar, and pulse until completely smooth. Adjust salt level.

9. Fill sterilized bottle with hot sauce. Keeps well refrigerated for at least 6 months.

Great Chefs, Great Wings: Ken Oringer on Wings

Ken Oringer has long been known as one of Boston's greatest chefs. The James Beard Award winner's flagship fine-dining spot Clio was routinely included in best-of lists (he closed it after nineteen years to focus on more casual food) and with his restaurants Uni, Toro, Coppa, and Little Donkey, Oringer has taken adventurous, creative approaches to Japanese, Barcelona-tapas, enoteca fare, and globally inspired small plates. But this renowned chef counts *Buffalo wings* as one of his "favorite things in the world."

Oringer told me he has probably served 100 different kinds of wings over the years and his knack for making them has caught the eye of national publications like *Food & Wine*. Clio's sticky glazed chicken wings with XO sauce and fried garlic garnered particular attention.

I caught up with Chef Oringer to get his wing philosophy and learn how to make kickass wings at home.

To double-fry or not to double-fry?

Chef Ken Oringer: I go back and forth with this: frying or baking, and then frying or double-frying, or no frying. It all depends on what texture you want, how crispy you want them, or how juicy you want them.

What's the deciding factor?

If you want to go with a flavorful sauce on top, you can give up the super juicy ones. You know, like Korean for instance, which I love. Korean wings are much juicier and crunchier. It's a completely different style. It's twice-cooked, sometimes even three times cooked. For an overall wing, like the ones we did at Clio, they were more or less always confited and then fried just so that we could get as much flavor into them as possible. They were brined and rubbed, cooked in duck fat, then cured for a couple days to ripen in the duck fat. Then we'd just warm them to remove the fat and throw them into a 375°F fryer.

What kind of oil is best for wings?

If you didn't have to worry about allergies, peanut oil. Or else cottonseed oil is really good. Many Japanese chefs will use grain oil or cottonseed oil to do their tonkatsu.* You can get it really crispy and clean at a high temperature.

Anything different oil-wise you have to do when cooking the confited wings?

The advantage of them being confited is that they're cooked already. They can go at a hotter cook temperature. And cottonseed oil you can fry really, really hot. They recuperate really nicely.

---

* Tonkatsu is a Japanese dish consisting of a breaded, deep-fried pork cutlet.

Any tips or tricks for home chefs?

If you're not going to confit, then definitely slow-cook them on a rack in an oven, well-seasoned on the first cook so that the skin won't be rubbery. You can start rendering some of the fat on the skin.

Why render?

That's the problem with wings. A lot of the times you're left with that rubbery fat. If you render them, you can start getting some of that fat to soften and even kind of cure it with a little bit of salt on a rack in the refrigerator overnight or for a couple of days to kind of dry it out, almost Peking duck-style. That always makes the wings crispier when you go to cook them a second time.

At Uni, you serve a dish called "Buffalo Mentaiko Spaghetti." What's that all about?

Buffalo wings are my favorite thing in the world. This is an homage to them. It's basically a ramen that's been blanched, heated with a Japanese Buffalo sauce that's like Frank's hot sauce, butter, and dashi. Then we put raw egg yolk on top and a ton of chiffonaded nori and scallions. It's kind of like a late-night izakaya type of dish. Really, really tasty.

You grew up in Paramus, New Jersey . . . how'd you become a wingnut?

When I grew up in the '80s was when bar food was getting its start, especially in New Jersey where deep-fried hot dogs were the scene. With a lot of these dive foods, there would be a certain place that served the best of each. When I was in junior high and cooking in some junky, old places, we would cook wings when Buffalo wings first got popular. I fell in love. Then it became something where you would go around to dive bars and see who would make the best ones. It was kind of a cult following.

To dip or not to dip?

You got to dip. That's the beauty of it. I don't do a heavy dip. I go light dip.

What's your go-to heat level?

Buffalo wings shouldn't be too spicy. Then you're going into something that's not a Buffalo wing. You've got to have Frank's sauce. It makes the best Buffalo wing. Anything that goes hotter, it's not a Buffalo wing. We do a habanero-jerk wing. It's delicious but it's not a Buffalo wing. I love Frank's. Frank's is what makes it for me. I don't think there's any hot sauce anywhere in the world that has more appeal.

PIT-Y-ROASTED THE FOOL

La Nova Pizzeria claims to have originated this style in the early 1970s. "I was fooling around with ribs one day," Joe Todaro Sr. told me. "We threw some wings on. The rest is history."

For the uninitiated, "from the pit," "over-the-pit," "off the pit," "Bar-B-Que," or just "BBQ" wings is *not* barbecue in the true, Texan-post-oak, low-and-slow meaning of the term, but it *is* a damned fine Yankee way of using a fires of hell-fueled grill to add another level of flavor (char, bitter, sweet) and texture (crispness and crunch) to Buffalo's signature dish.

While the menu terminology varies depending on the restaurant (and it still won't stop purists from rolling their eyes at a reference to grilling as "barbecue") the technique, frying, *then* grilling wings, and finally coating them with sweet and tangy barbecue sauce, is a standard if still relatively undeservedly uncelebrated way nationally of preparing Buffalo's signature dish.

OFF-THE-PIT BBQ BUFFALO WINGS

PREP TIME: 20 minutes ⋆ **COOKING TIME:** 1 hour ⋆ **YIELD:** 24 wings

2 dozen chicken wings cut into flats and
drumettes (about 2 pounds)
Kosher salt
Freshly ground black pepper
1 cup of your favorite store-bought or
homemade barbecue sauce

1. Preheat fryer (or a pot with enough oil to cover) to 350°F, and get grill smoking hot.

2. If not already done, cut off wingtips, and cut wing and drumstick at the joint. Dry wings thoroughly. Season wings with salt and pepper.

3. In batches of six, fry wings for 10 minutes. Drain, remove, and toss on the grill, leaving at least a wing's worth of space in between them. Cook 3 minutes and flip onto a hot, unused area of the grill. Cook another 3 minutes.

4. Remove wings to a large bowl and toss with barbecue sauce. Serve immediately.

RED SOX WINGS IN YANKEES COUNTRY?

Garlic Parmesan is a sauce you'll see on many a menu in Buffalo, but the combination of it with mild, medium, or hot sauce is a little rarer. In Buffalo, Bases Loaded and Wiechec's are two of the style's well-known practitioners, though they're only known by the "Red Sox" moniker at Wiechec's (Ernie Jewitt, the owner of Bases Loaded calls them "stinky wings").

Why Red Sox? Wiechec's is a Yankees bar and a Red Sox fan who works there invented them. He knew he'd come up with something so delicious that he could endlessly tweak Yankees fans, who wouldn't be able to stop themselves from ordering them.

Whatever you want to call them, when this cross-pollination happens, it's a must-order item. They're tangy and spicy with a consistent garlic presence and a mildly funky Parmesan cheesiness. Orders in this style are typically *especially* well-sauced, with a ratio of about two tablespoons of sauce to each wing—each wing should leave behind about a quarter- to a half-tablespoon of sauce on your fingers. They'll look like they've been confetti-coated with cheese, then coated thickly with butter and Frank's. In fact, you'll know you've added enough cheese when it's hard to imagine you could saturate it further without making paste.

RED SOX WING SAUCE
[GARLIC PARMESAN HOT WINGS]

PREP TIME: 3 minutes ★ **COOKING TIME:** 6 minutes ★ **YIELD:** About 2 cups sauce

⅔ cup butter

3 tablespoons finely minced garlic

1 cup Frank's RedHot Sauce

1 teaspoon garlic powder

1 teaspoon onion powder

2 tablespoons white vinegar

½ cup grated Parmesan

1. Melt butter in a saucepan over medium-low heat. Don't brown it!

2. Add garlic and warm over low heat 3 minutes.

3. Add hot sauce, garlic and onion powders, and vinegar. Whisk until well combined.

4. Remove from heat and transfer into a large bowl for tossing the wings. Add Parmesan and stir until thoroughly combined.

5. Toss coated wings in sauce, spoon some of the remaining sauce over them, and serve with blue cheese dressing and celery and/or carrots.

LAZINESS IS CLOSE TO GODLINESS

The buttermilk soak has long been a tenderizing step in the fried and roast chicken game (the general rule is eight hours to overnight), and it's made its way into corners of the wing recipe world. I'm just not sold it's necessary for great wings. That said, faced with some extra blue cheese dressing, inspired by Chef Marshal Grady, and channeling both my inner fat kid and obsessive-compulsive disorder, I came up with this much simpler version that solves a whole bunch of wing issues: blue cheese dressing sliding off well-dressed wings, that unappealing glop of hot sauce from wing dipping that turns a cup of dressing into a swirly soup,

and not getting enough dressing per wing after one bite.

I suppose you could serve extra ramekins of dressing for personal dipping (and double-dipping), but that makes for extra dishes. I love butter, but what about skipping it and compensating for losing that fat by just combining the hot sauce with blue cheese dressing then tossing the wings in that? You'd gain back the fat there, after all, right? Or, just *keep* the butter and mix wing sauce with blue cheese dressing. I mean, you have to be a blue cheese lover (can you really not be if you love wings?) but it turns out both work more than pretty damn well.

SPICY BLUE CHEESE BUFFALO SAUCE

PREP TIME: 1 minute ★ **YIELD:** 1 cup

½ cup Homemade Blue Cheese Dressing
½ cup Buffalo Wing Sauce

1. Mix. Toss. Eat. You're welcome.

CAN'T BELIEVE IT'S NOT BUTTER? IT'S NOT!

They say that authentic Buffalo wings (or chicken wings, as they say *in* the City of Good Neighbors) are made with Frank's RedHot and butter. That may have been true *everywhere* decades ago. Today? Not so much. Here's the dirty secret that many wing makers will cop to but are unlikely to volunteer: butter is expensive. To help offset expenses, restaurateurs often use a cheaper, butter-flavored *oil* substitute. One, called Whirl, is made with soybean oil and hydrogenated soybean oil (which many dieticians will tell you is a big no-no). I'm not

suggesting you use it—my rec is to *always* use butter. That being said, it's a safe bet that at least half of the wing places you visit anywhere *don't*, making that whole authenticity thing a tricky conversation. Interestingly, while most folks I tested preferred a sauce made with real butter, in a side-by-side sampling, only one in three was able to tell which was which. (It's a fun test—try it.)

That being said, using Whirl doesn't require any cooking, which *does* make wing life a little easier if you're throwing a party and making huge batches of wings in an increasingly inebriated state. (Here's where I say something snarky about it being okay to do if you don't care about the people you're making wings for. There, said it. Kidding! Kind of! But not really.) If you are going to use it, keep in mind that you can't use Whirl the same way you'd use butter, warming it on low heat, then adding Frank's. The resulting sauce won't emulsify and will run right off your wings, leaving them bereft of seasoning or flavor.

A recipe for Whirl wing sauce on its maker Stratas' website suggests an alternative that feels Frankenfood-ish in that instead of heat requires a half-hour wait. According to Stratas Foods, that allows the flavors to fully develop. Either way, the result is much thicker sauce. Their original recipe calls for two tablespoons of granulated garlic, a touch added by a chef for Stratas Foods, but that results in a gritty texture I didn't find in *any* sauce in Buffalo. I'd skip that, but follow the suggestion to add vinegar to bring out the flavor of the hot sauce.

WHIRL WING SAUCE

PREP TIME: 35 minutes (5 minutes active) ★ **YIELD:** 1¾ cups sauce

¼ **cup cider vinegar**

½ **cup Whirl**

1 cup The Original Louisiana Brand Hot Sauce

1. Combine all items and whisk together.

2. Allow to stand for 30 minutes before coating chicken wings.

BEEF ON WECK ROAST BEEF (PAGE 52)

BEEF ON WECK

◆———◆———◆

Great beef on weck isn't easy to pull off, which is probably why you haven't seen it take off across America. To do it right, you need to cook a large hunk of beef slowly (typically top round) and cut it tracing paper thin, and you need a fresh, salt-and-caraway studded roll called a *kummelweck*, or *weck*. That top round gets slow-roasted to medium-rare, then sliced thin and dipped in savory au jus to warm and juice it up before layering a huge pile of it inside the untoasted weck whose top is dipped in au jus before covering the beef. There are two advanced moves—cheese and gravy—but forgoing those, the most important thing is to have some freshly grated horseradish to pile on.

Schwabl's, Eckl's, Charlie the Butcher, Kelly's Korner, Bar Bill Tavern—these places serve sandwiches so good as to have expats planning stops on the way to or from the airport when visiting. These versions of beef on weck plant the seed in visitors that this time, when they go home, they're going to just go ahead and make them from scratch even though they won't have those Costanzo's rolls that help make them so good (most restaurants in Buffalo apply salt and caraway seeds to Costanzo's rolls with an egg or cornstarch wash). But hey, a few places make their own kummelweck, and that's something you'll probably want to do if you want to make a great version at home.

A ROLL BY ANY OTHER NAME . . .

I must have tested at least a dozen kummelweck roll recipes published online and collected from clippings in the food files at the research library at the Buffalo History Museum, and I have to say, I've had little delight at their success. To boot, the ones in the clippings weren't terribly straightforward. In the end, a riff on a recipe for dinner rolls I was directed to by Buffalo expat and chef Matthew Gunther (former sous chef at Gabriel Kreuther in Midtown Manhattan) worked best. I separated the salt from the yeast and reduced the amount of flour. And while I preferred using egg over cornstarch, I also have to side with John Marren of Brooklyn's outpost for Nickel City eats, Buffalo Famous, when it comes to making the salt-caraway mix stick to the rolls. As he said, "Our two cents is one whole egg, four whites, and a little water beats cornstarch any day."

A few handy shortcuts I found really helpful:

★ You want rolls wide enough to be sliced in half after the beef is layered on that won't topple over. If you want uniform rolls, spray the inside of six 8-ounce plastic deli containers, put the dough in, and press it down and up against the sides of the containers, *then* let it rise. Then just turn each container upside down!

★ You can uniformly scatter the seasoning on the bottom of a sheet tray and turn the glazed rolls *upside-down* on the mixture. It can make evenly coating them much easier.

★ When adhering the salt-caraway mixture to the rolls, remember the history of the sandwich and the reason why it was there in the first place (to make people drink more beer!) and that this is largely where much of the seasoning for the beef comes from.

★ These rolls freeze pretty well. You can keep them in sealable plastic bags and bring them back per the store-bought cheat in the pages to come.

Just remember, don't salt until you're really ready to use them or they'll dry out!

═══════ HOMEMADE KUMMELWECK ROLLS ═══════

PREP TIME: 2 hours and 30 minutes (30 minutes active) ★ **COOKING TIME:** 20 minutes ★
YIELD: 6 rolls

1½ **cups milk**

1½ **tablespoons butter, softened**

3 **teaspoons active dry yeast**

1 **tablespoon sugar**

3 **cups all-purpose flour**

1 **tablespoon kosher salt**

1 **egg**

3 **tablespoons pretzel salt**

3 **tablespoons caraway seeds**

1. Preheat oven to 425°F.

2. Combine milk and butter in a small saucepan over low heat until milk is just warm. Remove milk from heat to a mixing bowl.

3. Stir in yeast and sugar and let proof 5 minutes.

4. Combine flour and kosher salt.

5. Add yeast mixture to flour.

6. Using a mixer with a dough hook, or by hand, knead dough until smooth and completely combined, about 15 minutes. Place dough in a greased bowl and cover with plastic wrap. Let rise until dough doubles in size, about an hour.

7. Work air out of dough. Use a scale to divide into six portions. Form round balls, place them on a Silpat-lined baking sheet and let rise 30 minutes. Bake 15 minutes. Remove and let cool.

8. Scramble egg with fork to create wash. Separately, mix pretzel salt and caraway seeds.

9. Place rolls in an empty tray and coat entire top surface of each roll (you can dip a paper towel if you don't have a pastry brush). Sprinkle 1 to 2 teaspoons of salt-caraway mixture over each roll.

10. Return rolls to the oven 3 to 5 minutes, then serve!

BEEF (ON WECK)... IT'S WHAT'S FOR DINNER

You really need a nice hunk of meat to make good beef on weck, which makes this a great recipe for a party or a big dinner with lots of guests and not so much something you're going to make after work during the middle of the week. This recipe will make about eight to ten well-stacked sandwiches depending on how generous you are with the beef.

At trade shows, Charlie the Butcher (perhaps Buffalo's most well-known food personality, locally and nationwide) has recommended cooking the beef at 250°F, but if you don't have one of those fancy commercial Alto-Shaam ovens (I don't and I'm betting you don't either), 200°F should work just fine. Technically, you're going to want to check that the internal temperature reaches 120°F for medium rare, 130°F for medium, 135°F for medium-well, and 140°F for well-done. My advice though is to cook it to medium rare and then slice. Remember, you're going to be giving those juicy slices a bath in warm broth, so they'll get a little more cooked through again right before they go on the sandwich.

After all, you can't *uncook* the beef once it comes out of the oven, right?

BEEF ON WECK ROAST BEEF

PREP TIME: 25 to 30 minutes ★ **COOKING TIME:** 2 hours ★ **YIELD:** 6 sandwiches

Kosher salt

Freshly ground black pepper

1 teaspoon garlic powder

1 teaspoon onion powder

1 teaspoon dill seed powder

1 teaspoon coriander powder

1 teaspoon paprika

3¼ pounds top round

3 cups beef broth

6 kummelweck rolls

6 tablespoons fresh horseradish

6 dill pickle spears

1. Preheat oven to 200°F.

2. Combine seasoning in a small bowl, then rub to cover all sides of beef.

3. Cook at 200°F for about 2 hours, until internal temperature reaches 120°F for medium rare.

4. Rest roast 10 minutes.

5. Bring beef broth to a simmer in a small pot on stove, then turn off the heat.

6. Use a hollow-edge slicer or a *very* sharp carving knife to cut slices against grain as *thin* as possible. Weigh portions of 5 to 6 ounces per sandwich.

7. Slice rolls horizontally. Evenly layer roast beef on bottom. Quickly dip the underside of the top half of roll in the au jus (remember, like Charlie the Butcher says, "This is **not** a French dip!"), then top sandwich and slice in half.

8. Serve with fresh horseradish and a dill pickle spear.

BETTER THAN THE BOTTLED STUFF

Yes, you can buy horseradish at the store. And if you're in Buffalo, you should go get some of the famous stuff at Broadway Market, the city's custodian of its Eastern European food traditions. But there's also nothing like making the fresh variety yourself. And it's *so* easy.

Keep in mind that *when* you add the vinegar is important. That distinct taste we humans dig so much was actually developed by the horseradish plant as a natural defense against predators. Not

to get too science-y, but when it's grated, enzymes from the plant's cells break down a glucosinolate called sinigrin to produce a compound called allyl isothiocyanate. Us non-science folks know that as mustard oil.

This is all to say that the longer that chemical reaction goes without being inhibited, the more intense the effect (and incentive for the interloping predator to beg off). So if you like your horseradish mild, add the vinegar right away. If you like it hot, wait three minutes. You know you're gonna wait now, aren't you? Yeah, you are. I knew it.

The amount of horseradish that should be applied to beef on weck is personal preference, but a tablespoon per sandwich spread evenly over the beef should do the trick (even with a three-minute wait on that vinegar).

Oh, and be careful breathing over the blender while it's chopping. That's a strong whiff!

EASY HOMEMADE HORSERADISH

PREP TIME: 15 minutes (10 minutes active) ★ **YIELD:** About 1 cup

1 horseradish root
Distilled white vinegar (about ½ to 1 cup)
½ teaspoon kosher salt

1. Peel horseradish and cut out any blemishes. Cut root into 1-inch cubes.

2. Pulse in a blender until horseradish is chopped into fine threads.

3. If you like it hot, let horseradish breath for 3 to 5 minutes to let flavor and strength develop. Otherwise, add immediately.

4. Place shredded horseradish into a sealable container, add vinegar to cover and salt. Stir well and test seasoning. If horseradish is too pungent you can add water a tablespoon at a time to dilute it.

5. Place mixture in a small glass jar and screw lid on firmly. Store in fridge for up to 6 weeks, or up to 6 months in freezer.

FECKLESS IS AS WECKLESS DOES: BEEF ON WECK CHEATS

The kummelweck recipe in this book is pretty straightforward, but baking isn't for everyone. The measurements, yeast (what was the difference between active dry and compressed again?), the double-rise. Guh. But don't give up. You can get close by cheating. In a little under an hour you can use these cheats to make an easier version. Without a Tom & Jerry or a Labatt, you won't quite transport yourself to the city's best spots, but you can close your eyes and get pretty close. Doctor up some Kaiser rolls from your local supermarket, buy thinly shaved roast beef from its deli counter (and just warm it up in a little beef broth), and pile on your favorite brand of jarred horseradish.

Remember though, you're looking for an actual roast, not cold-cuts (it won't be as juicy). And since you'll be warming up the beef, ask for the rarest cut they have (you don't want to overcook it). All you need is a steamy hot oven to reanimate the rolls and an egg wash or cornstarch solution to adhere the salt and caraway. Dunk the beef in warm broth (not boiled or boiling!) for 30 seconds, dip the under-side of the roll top, pile on the horseradish, and "Let's-Go-Buff-A-Lo!"

I won't tell if you won't.

EASY BEEF ON WECK

PREP TIME: 35 minutes (25 minutes active) ★ **YIELD:** 4 sandwiches

4 **Kaiser rolls**

1 **egg**

2 **tablespoons pretzel salt**

2 **tablespoons caraway seeds**

1½ **cups beef broth**

1¼ **pounds thinly shaved roast beef**

4 **tablespoons store-bought grated horseradish**

1. Preheat oven to 425°F. Place a flat pan filled with steaming hot water in bottom of oven.

2. Run each roll under a running faucet for 2 seconds then pat dry with a towel.

3. Use same technique as described on page 50 in full recipe for applying egg wash and salt-caraway mixture to each roll top.

4. Warm rolls in oven 5 to 10 minutes. Meanwhile, warm beef broth in a small pot on stove. (It should be hot but not boiling.)

5. Dip beef in broth about 30 seconds. Meanwhile, slice rolls. Right before you're ready to serve, pile beef on bottom halves, dunk underside of each roll, pile on horseradish, cover with roll tops, and serve!

"This is Not a French Dip!" Charlie the Butcher on the Right Amount of Au Jus

If you think you know someone more Buffalo famous, Charlie the Butcher might have something to say about that. He's been on ABC's *Good Morning America*, *Live with Regis and Kathie Lee*, Food Network's *FoodNation with Bobby Flay*, and made numerous personal appearances across the country and around the world. And au jus runs through this man's veins—he follows his father Charles J. and his grandfather Charles E. Roesch, who founded the company in 1914 (and who was the city's mayor from 1930 to 1934). If you know Charlie, you know his signature look—a Charlie the Butcher–emblazoned apron and his classic white bump cap—which he's been donning since his 1984 debut at a trade show.

Why hasn't beef on weck become more of a nationally known sandwich?

Charlie the Butcher: You need a national chain like Applebee's or Chili's to pick it up and take it out of here and make it famous. I've gone to Texas, Charlotte, Florida, New York City, and Tampa to show people how to make it, but it hasn't gone national.

Is there anything else that prevents this specialty from spreading outside Western New York?

The rolls need to have a clean flavor and have to hold up to the beef. We use Costanzo's rolls. You can't ship those rolls because the salt dries out the bread.

What cut do you use to make beef on weck?

We use top round. It's the single leanest muscle, but we tenderize and age it overnight.

How much meat goes on each sandwich?

We serve four to five ounces of meat per sandwich.

Any advice for those who want to make it at home?

We sell our meat in a one-pound packet with au jus. You just heat the au jus up to 160°F to 175°F and dip the roast beef in it for 30 seconds. The roll is basically a Kaiser roll so you can pick up a few of them, brush the tops of them with a little cornstarch solution, sprinkle a little of our caraway-salt mixture on top, and then heat them in a 350°F oven for four minutes.

What's the right amount of au jus for great beef on weck?

I think one of the keys here is the understated nature of the roll. It should be a quality roll, fresh but not too much texture, seasoning to help with the flavor. And then not too much wetness! This is *not* a French dip. It shouldn't be sopping, just a little wet on the underside. If the meat isn't moist, you're not going to save it with a sopping wet bun.

Charlie, you're an institution in Buffalo, but what are some of *your* picks for the city's great food institutions?

Brennan's for wings. Bocce and La Nova for pizza. Hutch's for their bone-in filet. And Glen Park Tavern for haddock.

CHICKEN FINGER SUB (PAGE 64)

BUFFALO FAMOUS

Other Iconic Buffalo Dishes (a.k.a. Food Buffalebrities)

◆——————◆——————◆

Buffalo isn't *just* about wings. There's also a great hot dog tradition, from Greek-originated "Texas red hots." And it's a city of great sandwiches, where capicola gets layered on grilled sausage, and sautéed dandelion greens top "steak in the grass," and where chicken fingers slip off children's menus and into soft Costanzo's sub rolls with provolone, tomato, lettuce, blue cheese dressing, and Frank's RedHot Sauce to become something *naughty*. It's a town where the darkest, salt-of-the-earth bar has bartenders who make epic steak and bologna sandwiches between pouring shots. A city with carving stations *dedicated* to beef on weck, which should be up there with Pittsburgh's Primanti Bros., Los Angeles's French dip at Philippe the Original, and pastrami at Katz's in New York City.

Speaking of New York City, Buffalo has just as intense of a pizza culture and a tradition that goes back as far as at least 1927. It's a style made for bracing against the cold of football tailgating. And its Italian food traditions don't stop there. There are Russian roulette–spicy banana peppers bursting with cheese and bowls of lightly sauced spaghetti parm covered with a thick, melted layer of mozzarella that guarantees a cheese-pull every time. Not only that, but Buffalo is a city with a food schedule and calendar. On Fridays, religion sometimes intersects with wings, when the Catholic-inspired fish fry tradition means no wings until the fryer oil can be changed after dinner. And it guarantees to keep its secrets unless you go to certain places on certain days during different times of year. Consider sponge candy, a chocolate-covered toffee made with baking soda, and whose inside looks a little like a Butterfinger but tastes nothing like it. There's the Brigadoon sardine-studded *pasta con sarde* that's green with fennel, red with tomato paste, and only appears on March 19th during the Sicilian feast of San Giuseppe (St. Joseph). Then there's the Tom & Jerry, a seasonally available frothy, rum-and-brandy-soaked cocktail laboriously made with eggs, whose whites and yolks are whipped separately and folded together with sugar and spice, ladled out of a punch bowl on the back of the bar, meticulously layered according to the rules of the house, and subject to long drinking sessions frequently tied to the intensity of the weather. Imagine the best eggnog you've ever had and it doesn't even come close to how good this drink is.

Spinach loaf, stinger tacos, pierogi, pizza logs—read on for the recipes to make your food Buffalebrity dreams come true.

AMERICA'S MOST UNDERRATED REGIONAL PIZZA STYLE?

I've eaten at many of America's most well-respected pizzerias, and I'm going to put a decade of pizza cred built by writing about and visiting hundreds of pizzerias, and say that Buffalo-style pizza is this country's most underappreciated regional style. My Manhattan pizza friends can shake their heads. Buffalo has awesome pizza. I'm in love.

For those who haven't had the pleasure, Buffalo-style pizza is *not* Buffalo chicken pizza (a long story). It's been described as a hybrid of Chicago deep-dish and New York or somewhere between Detroit's airy, high-lipped cheesy crust and New York City's traditionally thin-crust pies. It's also been characterized as a circular version of Sicilian, but Buffalo style's undercarriage is softer and its signature sweet sauce is completely different.

I'd flip the description. Buffalo-style pizza is a cup-and-char pepperoni pizza, one with a slim, sometimes nonexistent crust coastline with ingredients out to and sometimes even *over* the edges, with a thick, airy undercarriage with little to no structural integrity that's topped by a sweet sauce and enough cheese to nearly *always* guarantee a cheese-pull. If you were going to use other regional styles to

describe it, I'd say there's a Detroit amount of cheese with a Motor City trim, a Maine undercarriage (think Micucci's or Slab), and a New York City soul.

La Nova, Bocce Club Pizza, and Bob & John's La Hacienda are three of Buffalo's most famous pizzerias, and Santora's, founded in 1927, is its oldest. And once you visit these places and get a taste for the style, it's easy to get hooked. Problem is, you can't really find Buffalo-style pizza in other cities (though I'd argue that New York City's most Instagrammed slice, Prince Street Pizza, is essentially Buffalo style squared).

That's a problem.

Pizza can be a notoriously tough thing to replicate at home where you don't have the dry, high heat of a deck oven and its hot, hot, hot floor. And there's very little written in books or online that I could find about the ingredients and ratio needed to make Buffalo pizza dough. So I promised myself early on that I wasn't going to try. But the longer I went, the more I jonesed. Finally, temptation became too much. At that point, even a copy of a facsimile would do.

After talking with many of Buffalo's best pizzeria owners, it's clear there are two ingredients vital to the dough: shortening and sugar. But everyone zipped up when it came to secret ingredient ratios for dough. So I reached out to a pizza maker known for his expertise in regional American pizza styles: Tony Gemignani.

Tony isn't from Buffalo (don't hold it against him) but he told me he's friendly with the Todaro family (which still owns and operates La Nova), and his book *The Pizza Bible* features recipes for more styles than you've probably ever heard of (his restaurant, Pizza Rock, may serve even more). "The low hydration, shortening, dense dough, and specific ingredients used such as the thick tomato paste sauce and hand-cut pepperoni, makes this style a special one," Tony explained to me.

I have Tony to thank for working with me on dough hydration (flour/liquid ratio). Funny story: after I'd finished honing the recipe, someone who has family ties to one of Buffalo's longstanding pizzerias reached out with photos of their heirloom recipes for dough and sauce. The dough recipe was just fractions of an ounce different in a few places! I'm proud to say this is a recipe whose end result you could squint at and feel the Lake-effect snow.

You'll want a stand mixer (to make the dough), a pizza steel (most stones aren't big enough—I recommend Modernist Cuisine's), and an 18-inch or 20-inch pizza pan depending on which style you're making. Your pie should be the same size either way, but if you're making it Bocce style, you need to use the larger pan to allow the cheese, sauce, and pepperoni to be distributed right over the edge of the crust.

Lastly, you should also order pepperoni, preferably from a company called Margherita, which 90 percent of Buffalo's pizzerias use (you can find it on Amazon or Buffalo Foods). Other legit substitutes to achieve classic Buffalo cup-and-char (curled up, black-rimmed cups filled with spicy pepperoni oil) are Battistoni, Ezzo, and Vermont Smoke & Cure (failing that, buy Hormel and hand-slice it). You want slices slightly thicker than 1/8 inch. Now, let's make some pizza pies.

BUFFALO PIZZA DOUGH

PREP TIME: 25 hours (15 minutes active) ✶ **YIELD:** 2 dough balls

0.24 ounce active dry yeast

28.8 ounces warm water (80 to 85°F)

3 pounds (48 ounces) high-gluten flour

0.96 ounce sugar

0.96 ounce sea salt

1.4 ounces shortening

1. Add yeast to a large bowl. Add water and whisk to blend. Pour into stand mixer bowl. Add flour and mix on slow. Sprinkle in sugar. After 2 minutes add salt. You may have to stop and scrape the sides to help dough come together. Restart mixer. After 2 more minutes, add shortening and mix 3 minutes.

2. Remove dough to a clean bowl, cover with a clean damp cloth, and let rise for 45 minutes. Cut into two balls, place on a cookie sheet, cover with plastic wrap, and refrigerate for 24 hours.

3. Take dough out 1 hour before use.

BUFFALO PIZZA SAUCE

PREP TIME: 5 minutes ✶ **COOKING TIME:** 15 minutes ✶
YIELD: 2 cups sauce (enough for two 18-inch pizzas)

3 teaspoons extra virgin olive oil

1 ounce tomato paste

1 cup water

1 teaspoon garlic powder

1 teaspoon onion powder

½ teaspoon dried oregano

½ teaspoon dried basil (or
   minced fresh)

¼ teaspoon freshly ground black pepper

2 teaspoons sugar

1 teaspoon kosher salt

1. Add olive oil to a large saucepan on low heat. Add tomato paste and water. Stir to thoroughly combine.

2. Add the rest of the ingredients, stir to combine, and simmer for 10 minutes. Turn off heat and let cool.

BUFFALO PIZZA

PREP TIME: 1 hour and 20 minutes (20 minutes active) ✶ **COOKING TIME:** 20 minutes ✶
YIELD: Two 18-inch pizzas

1 cup bench flour

2 rounds Buffalo Pizza Dough (see
   recipe above)

8 teaspoons shortening

2 cups Buffalo Pizza Sauce (see recipe above)

42 ounces shredded mozzarella

4 teaspoons olive oil (optional)

⅔ cup sesame seeds, onion powder, garlic powder, Cajun spice, or Parmesan (optional)

1 pound sliced pepperoni (preferably Margherita)

1. Preheat oven to its highest setting, preferably 550°F. Place pizza steel in the oven. After it reaches 550°F, keep oven closed for 1 hour.

2. If you have advanced pizza dough moves, this is where to show them off. If you don't, cheat. Generously dust dough "bench" with flour (about ½ cup). Turn one dough round in on itself underneath to form a ball. Press down in the center and push out toward the edges repeatedly while also moving the dough in a circle clockwise for 15 seconds. Lift dough, dust the surface with flour, flip dough, then stretch from the center out to the edge while turning the dough in a circle for 2 minutes, and forming a slightly raised lip. Repeat until pizza is as wide as the pan and even throughout beyond the edge.

3. Use a paper towel to grease the entire surface of an 18-inch pizza pan with shortening (4 teaspoons). Place dough on pan and stretch out to arrange it so it reaches out a hair shy of the pan's edge.

4. Ladle up to 1 cup of sauce from the center out in a spiral until it's evenly spread out over the dough up to ¼ inch of the edge. If you're making it Bocce Club style, ladle the sauce over the edge of the crust.

5. Evenly spread 21 ounces of cheese over the sauced dough. If you're making it Bocce style, let the cheese cover the entire surface of the dough, including the crust. If you're making it La Nova style, leave the crust rim cheese-free. You can either leave things at that or brush optional olive oil (2 teaspoons per pizza) along the rim and sprinkle sesame seed, onion powder, garlic powder, Cajun spice, or Parmesan on the crust ½ inch from the edge toward the center all the way around.

6. Evenly distribute half the pepperoni so that when you cut the pie in 8 slices there are 10 to 13 slices of pepperoni on each one. If there doesn't seem to be room, just do your best to pile them in between each other—the pepperoni will shrink as it cooks and things will fall into place. Don't worry if things don't look exactly symmetrical. Controlled cup-and-char chaos is the effect you're going for. If you're making it Bocce style, make sure you have some pepperoni on the cornicione!

7. Place pan in oven for 10 minutes. Slide pizza off pan onto the steel and cook 2 to 3 minutes. Slide pie back onto the pan, cut into 8 slices, and serve.

8. Repeat for the second pie.

HEY KID, THOSE ARE *MY* CHICKEN FINGERS

This is *the* quintessential non-weck Buffalo sandwich, largely credited as being invented at Tonawanda's John's Pizza & Subs. John's co-owner Gene Mongan said it was something he made for himself to eat while working in kitchens in 1977, when the "chicken finger was new in the area," and that he and his partners put it on the menu at John's in 1982. Theirs is filled with fingers shaken in hot sauce, topped with lettuce, tomato, and provolone, then smothered with blue cheese.

This isn't a difficult sandwich to make by any means. It's finding the right kind of roll outside of Buffalo that's tricky. This *isn't* a crusty sandwich—you want a roll that's a little sweet and fairly squishy.

Not everyone in Buffalo makes their own blue cheese dressing. And those who do aren't typically keen on sharing the ratio of ingredients. That's okay—I do share.

One place where I diverge when I make the sandwich at home is the actual tenders. John Marren of Buffalo's Famous in New York City, one of the places *outside* Buffalo that gets it right, insists that you *really* just should be using frozen food–aisle chicken tenders or tenderloins. "They have to look pressed flat and be deep-fried," he told me.

And he's right that that's likely the kind of product that many places in Buffalo use. But I'm a bit hard-headed, and usually go ahead and make my own with the best chicken I can find. You're welcome to use the store-bought stuff, of course. If you decide to go the homemade route, just make sure to cut or pound your tenders to make sure they're flat (for stacking).

═══ CHICKEN FINGER SUB ═══

PREP TIME: 20 minutes ★ **COOKING TIME:** 15 minutes ★ **YIELD:** 1 sandwich

½ cup Buffalo Wing Sauce (page 22)

4 boneless, skinless chicken breast
   tenderloins

⅓ cup flour

1 egg, beaten

½ cup bread crumbs (or Buffalo Bread
   Crumbs, page 98)

1 soft white hoagie roll

½ cup Homemade Blue Cheese Dressing
   (page 38)

4 leaves iceberg lettuce (shredding optional)

2 thin slices tomato

4 thin slices red onion

1. Prep Buffalo Wing Sauce.

2. Evenly coat chicken fingers on all sides first in flour, then egg, then bread crumbs.

3. Preheat fryer or skillet filled with enough oil to cover the fingers. Carefully release the chicken fingers into the oil. Cook 3 to 5 minutes until golden brown (not dark!), then remove to a drying rack or paper towels.

4. Meanwhile, open roll and toast until slightly golden. Slather inside of top and bottom with Blue Cheese Dressing. Create a layer of lettuce on top of that, pile on the tomato, and finish with the red onion.

5. Toss fingers in wing sauce to completely cover, then stack them on the bed of lettuce, tomato, and onion.

6. Top with the roll half, slice on a bias, and serve.

FRIED FISH AND CHIPS: AS EASY AS FRY

It's been said that the hardest thing about making a good fish fry is coordinating your fries and your fish because they're both best right after they're fried and they both need to be cooked at different temperatures. Your fish, the thinking goes, needs to be fried at 350°F for about seven minutes, and the French fries need to fry at 375°F for 10 to 15 minutes (depending on the cut).

I dunno, it doesn't sound like a terribly big deal to me to pre-fry the fries first and set them aside, then fry the fish and drop the fries in the oil quickly to warm them up right before serving; but to make

this easy as can be, I like to use my adapted version of *New York Times* food writer Julia Moskin's cold-oil method. With this, making the fries is just a matter of tossing them in a large pot with oil and turning the dial from low to medium.

That out of the way, there's the matter of dredge versus batter. There's something to be said for the old-school dredge, and it's easier, but I'm a fan of beer batter. You get that crispy crust whose contrast to the juicy flakes of steaming hot fish make the dish all the more enjoyable.

Pro-Tip: McDonald's French fries were once known for being so tasty because they were fried in beef tallow (rendered beef fat). Try adding some bacon to your oil—it's the same idea. You may be surprised by how tasty the fries come out.

FISH FRY

PREP TIME: 65 minutes ★ **COOKING TIME:** 1 hour ★ **SERVES:** 4 people

7 large Idaho potatoes

2 strips bacon (optional)

1 gallon peanut oil (or your favorite vegetable oil)

¾ cup rice flour

1½ cups white flour

1 teaspoon baking powder

1 teaspoon sugar

½ cup soda water

¾ cup lager

Kosher salt

2 pounds haddock or cod, cut in four pieces

1. Peel potatoes and slice lengthwise, about ½-inch thick. Keeping the slices stacked,

continued

slice again at the same thickness to cut your fries. Soak in cold water for 30 minutes.

2. Drain fries and dry thoroughly with a towel. Add optional bacon strips to a large pot, add potatoes, and cover with oil so the tops of the fries are an inch below the surface. Turn heat to the lowest setting and cook until soft (30 minutes), stirring once in a while to prevent sticking. You're going to crisp the fries up later, while you're frying the fish.

3. For the fish, set your fryer to 350°F or add 2 inches of vegetable oil to an additional large heavy pot and bring up to that heat, checking temperature with a thermometer.

4. To make the beer batter: In a large bowl, add the rice flour, 1 cup of the white flour, the baking powder, and sugar. Add soda water, beer, and salt. Mix until thoroughly combined and smooth, but don't overmix. Pour remaining ½ cup of white flour in a container or tray big enough to hold a piece of fish. Toss one piece of fish at a time in the flour to coat on all sides.

5. Turn heat on the French fries up to medium and fry them until crisp (10 to 15 minutes). Meanwhile, line a baking tray with paper towels to dry off excess oil.

6. Drop a piece of fish in batter to coat completely, then remove and gently lower into the oil. Repeat immediately with a second piece of fish. Cook both 7 minutes, then remove to a tray lined with paper towels. Repeat with next two pieces of fish.

7. Drain fries, toss in a tray lined with paper towels, and season with salt. Serve one piece fish and 2 cups fries per person.

BOLOGNA, BUFFALO STYLE

Bologna. It's cheap, accessible, has a long shelf life, and is frequently associated with German immigration. Is it any surprise then that Buffalo, with its blue-collar dynamic and German community, has a strong bologna tradition? And yes, while it still wears the stink of primary school, bologna is undergoing a resurgence, garnering attention from acclaimed chefs *outside* Buffalo who have rediscovered its potential and old-school appeal. That's nice, but in Buffalo, bologna never *went* anywhere. It's on most sandwich shop and pizzeria menus, cold with cheese, lettuce, and tomato, but usually also hot, fried, and topped with sautéed or grilled onions and/or peppers and melted white American cheese.

In Buffalo, Toutant, The Old Pink, and Sophia's may make the three best bologna sandwiches. While the core idea remains central to all three, they're different experiences. I particularly love the grilled one at The Pink, but there's something about Chef James Roberts' scratch version at Toutant, served on homemade hamburger rolls and topped with Genesee-soaked onions, that's haunting. And while you may not be rushing home to make your own bologna from scratch (or rolls for that matter), you *can* make a *really* deli-

cious version of his sandwich at home if you follow a few rules.

First, cold bologna? Slice it thin. Hot? Go thick. Ask your local butcher or deli guy to cut you a few ½-inch to ¾-inch thick slices. Avoid the classic mistake of overcooking the bologna. Fry the slices up low and slow in butter. And go heavy on the cheese. The result? A few thick griddled slices whose surfaces get caramelized with crispy edges while staying soft and warm inside. Draped with gooey cheese, covered with soft, sweet onions, and tucked into a soft, squishy roll, it can be a transformational moment.

FRIED BOLOGNA SANDWICH

PREP TIME: 15 minutes ★ **COOKING TIME:** 1 hour and 30 minutes ★ **YIELD:** 2 sandwiches

4 slices ½-inch or ¾-inch thick bologna (oh, just go big)

5 tablespoons butter

1 large white onion, sliced thin

1 green pepper, sliced thin (optional)

½ cup Genesee beer

continued

Kosher salt

Freshly ground black pepper

8 slices white American cheese

2 Kaiser rolls

4 tablespoons mayonnaise (for homemade, page 100)

1. Take bologna out of the refrigerator and let it reach room temperature.

2. In a large saucepan, melt 3 tablespoons butter over low heat. Add onions (and peppers, if you'd like), cover, and simmer 10 minutes, tossing occasionally to coat in butter, cooking until soft and translucent.

3. Add beer to onions and simmer, covered, for at least a half hour.

4. In another large pan, melt the remaining 2 tablespoons butter over low heat. Season all sides of bologna slices with salt and

pepper. Turn the heat down to the lowest setting, place the bologna slices in the pan, cover and let it cook gently for 8 minutes, occasionally spooning melted butter from the pan over the top of the slices.

5. Flip slices and cover each with two slices of white American cheese. Cover and let it all cook gently 8 more minutes.

6. Meanwhile, wrap the Kaiser rolls in damp paper towels and microwave them for 20 seconds. Slice in half, open, and toast until the surface starts to get just a little warm and crispy.

7. Spread mayonnaise on the insides of the tops and bottoms of the rolls. Layer two cheese-topped slices inside each roll, top with sautéed onions and optional peppers, close up the sandwiches, slice them down the center, and serve.

NA ZDROWIE, PIEROGI

In 1890, Buffalo's Polish-American population was estimated at 20,000. By 1910, it was 80,000 (about a sixth of its population) and there were *five* Polish-language newspapers. Today, the newspapers are gone, and the greatest concentration of Polish-Americans can likely be found in Buffalo's eastern suburbs (Cheektowaga and Marilla). Polish-Americans still make up about 10 percent of the city's total population and there are lots of places to experience the cuisine, whose most easily identifiable dishes are golabki (a.k.a. golombki) and pierogi.

In Buffalo, R&L is a poster child for Polish old-school Buffalo cuisine. "R&L" stands for Ronnie and Lottie—Ronnie and Lottie Pikuzinski, that is, the couple who have been running this local tavern since 1969, and married since 1957. And it's likely that unless you visit on one of the occasions where the whole neighborhood comes out, you may just be spending the afternoon with Ronnie and Lottie at the bar by yourself and whomever you go with. It's almost like visiting grandma and grandpa. The menu is simple: pierogi, "golompki" (golabki), hand-cut fries, and chicken fingers daily. Fish fry on Friday. That's all, folks. But these are

quite possibly going to be the best pierogi you'll ever have.

Sitting at the bar with Ronnie and Lottie took me back to my own Polish grandmother's kitchen, where I first learned how to make pierogi. And Lottie's are the closest I've come to tasting anything like Grandma Helen's since. *Na zdrowie* (bless you), Lottie. But trying to get Lottie Pikuzinski to give you a recipe for pierogi channels the frustration of all grown grandchildren trying to preserve family food traditions everywhere. There are barely any measurements, and no matter how good your pierogi end up being, they'll never taste as good as hers.

Watching Lottie make pierogi means guessing at how much flour she just dumped in from the bag leftover from last time. Still, there *is* rhyme and reason. Unlike store-bought spring roll wrappers, which can sometimes stand in credibly for ravioli, this dumpling dough is something you'll want to make from scratch. Fortunately, the recipe is simple (some recipes call for adding sour cream and butter to the dough—not Lottie's), and it's as close as you'll get to Lottie's unless you go to R&L.

She rolls them out really thin and long and none of them are the same size. They're amoeba-shaped if anything, which should make you pretty comfortable knowing you can't really get the shapes wrong. Seal them well, and just remember, she only barely fills them. That makes them light and enjoyable instead of the gut-bombs some pierogi can be.

LOTTIE'S PIEROGI AND BUFFALO WING PIEROGI

PREP TIME: 2 hours ★ **COOKING TIME:** 30 minutes ★ **YIELD:** 1 dozen pierogi

FOR THE FILLING:

Kosher salt

3 Yukon Gold potatoes, peeled and cubed

Freshly ground black pepper

2 eggs, whipped

2 cups farmer's cheese

FOR THE DOUGH:

3 eggs

1½ cups water

4½ cups unbleached all-purpose flour

COOK AND SERVE:

½ to 1 cup butter, as needed

16 ounces sour cream

1. For the filling: Bring a large pot of water to a boil. Salt water until it tastes like the ocean. Add peeled, cubed potatoes and cook 15 minutes. Remove potatoes without dumping the water—you'll reuse it later.

2. Mash potatoes in a large bowl or container until broken but not completely smooth, then remove and reserve in the fridge until no longer warm. Add whipped eggs and farmer's cheese, thoroughly mix, add salt and pepper to taste.

3. For the dough: Whisk or blend three eggs with equal amount of water (about 1½ cups water). Pour 3½ cups flour into a large bowl (or onto a flat surface if you're brave). Reserve remainder as board flour

(for rolling and keeping your rolling pin dry). Make a well in the center of the flour big enough to hold the entire egg-water mixture. Pour the mixture into the well, then use a fork to combine with the flour until the liquid disappears. Next, fold the dough until completely combined but don't overwork it. (If you're using a stand mixer, start on low for a minute, then mix at medium speed 4 to 5 minutes until the dough pulls away from the sides of the bowl.) Remove and reserve.

4. To assemble: Using a scale, divide dough into 24 (7-ounce) balls (or eyeball them like Lottie). You need two for each pierogi.

5. Roll two balls out flat, about 4 inches long and up to 3 inches wide, with a rolling pin or bottle (or, if you're fancy, a pasta machine). Put 1 teaspoon filling in the center of the bottom piece and spread it out evenly, leaving ¼ inch clear along the edge. Drape the top piece over the filling and crimp or press along the sides all the way around. (Lottie presses and doesn't use an egg wash or water to seal.) Eliminate as much air as possible while sealing. Set on a floured surface until ready to cook. Repeat until the dough's gone.

6. To cook: Use potato water if you didn't dump it; otherwise bring a large pot of water to a boil, then salt it. Gently lower four to six pierogi into water and cook until they float (about 2 minutes).

7. Warm a large saucepan over medium-low heat. Add butter and melt completely. Add three to four pierogi at a time to pan and cook until mottled with golden-brown patches, about 2 minutes on each side. Repeat as needed. Serve three to five per person with a large dollop of sour cream.

Note: You can lay pierogi out flat without touching and in layers separated with wax paper in a large sealable bag and store in the freezer up to 2 months.

Buffalo-ize it! To make Buffalo-ized pierogi, use Lottie's recipe to make the dough, then fill the pierogi using the recipe for Buffalo Chicken Pimento Cheese Salad (page 151). Cook them the same way as the other pierogi, but garnish with Blue Cheese Sour Cream (page 95).

THE BEST GARLIC CHEESE BREAD YOU'LL EVER HAVE

Oliver's Restaurant on Delaware Avenue is quintessential Buffalo fine dining with a history that goes back to 1936, when it was opened by Frank Oliver. By their estimation, during the decade Chef Mike Andrzejewski and his wife Sherri worked there, they prepared more than 120,000 spinach loaves. Chef Andrzejewski (who bested Bobby Flay on the Food Network star's show of *Beat Bobby Flay*) credits Oliver's legendary restaurateur Henry Gorino (its owner from 1983 until David Schutte took over in 2013) for the restaurant's recipe and popularity. And while Oliver's has the updated touches of modern tasting menus, the spinach loaf (beloved by customers and given the side-eye by some chefs) remains an indelible menu item.

"To make a proper spinach loaf, the starting point is the bread," Chef A notes. "In particular, you need a good Italian loaf, more of a sandwich-style or sub bread. Long and narrow, as opposed to a dinner loaf that you would serve with spaghetti. The crust-to-bread ratio is important. In Buffalo,

the favorites are Luigi's Family Bakery and Balistreri's, but some supermarkets make very acceptable breads also."

Chef A says grated Parmesan, Asiago, or Pecorino Romano will work (provolone too), adding that a blend can be even tastier. As for the spinach? "You can use quality frozen spinach, just defrost and squeeze out as much liquid as possible. If you choose fresh spinach, use the baby stuff so you don't have to pick the stems. Then wash and sauté it in butter until very tender, but again, be very sure to squeeze out as much excess juice as possible."

Lastly, the amount of butter and cheese in this recipe is *truly* impressive. It almost might be even more extreme than Oliver's own. If you need to, redistribute some of the cheese and spinach halfway through baking. I found the amounts work with a foot-long loaf (three to four inches wide and two inches tall) and that setting it overnight in the fridge (rolled tightly in plastic wrap) lets you keep the toppings evenly distributed. It'll just look like a butter submarine when you remove it from the fridge and you'll need to slice it open again with a knife!

OLIVER'S SPINACH LOAF

PREP TIME: 25 minutes ✶ **COOKING TIME:** 22 to 32 minutes ✶ **YIELD:** 1 loaf

1 cup grated Asiago

1 cup grated Parmesan

1 cup grated provolone

2 cups unsalted butter

1 cup onions, minced very fine

4 tablespoons minced fresh garlic

Kosher salt

Freshly ground black pepper

1½ pounds fresh baby spinach, cleaned thoroughly (or one 10-ounce package frozen spinach)

One 12-inch soft Italian sesame-studded roll

1. Preheat oven to 400°F.

2. Combine the cheeses thoroughly, then divide into three portions and set aside.

3. Warm a pot over medium heat, then add 2 cups butter. Once it's melted, remove 3 tablespoons of butter and reserve. Add the onions to stovetop butter and cook until onions are clear and tender, but not browned (about 3 minutes). Add garlic and cook 2 minutes. Salt and pepper to taste, but remember, the cheese will add salt too! Reserve at room temperature until you're ready to assemble the loaf.

4. If you're using frozen spinach, defrost, wrap in paper towels, then squeeze until dry. If you're using *fresh* spinach, warm a saucepan over medium heat, then add 3 tablespoons of the butter-onion mixture to the spinach and cook until completely wilted. When cool, wrap in paper towels and squeeze until dry. Gently toss spinach with 2 tablespoons butter-onion mixture to flavor it.

5. Slice the loaf in half lengthwise without cutting it all the way through as if you were making a sandwich with a hinge. Fold it completely open flat (you might want to do this over a foil-lined sheet tray or on a cutting board!).

6. Think layers! Spread half of the butter-onion mixture thoroughly across the face of both sides of the open bread. Sprinkle a third of the cheese mixture over the top. Cover the entire surface of the open bread with spinach out to the edges. Sprinkle another third of of cheese mixture evenly over the top (don't be shy). Cover the surface of the cheese-covered spinach with the remaining butter-onion mixture. Evenly sprinkle half of the remaining third cheese over the spinach, then fold the bread closed.

7. "This next part sounds trivial," Chef Mike says, "but is key to a good loaf! This will give you the texture that will make a superior spinach loaf when baked." Using the reserved 3 tablespoons butter, brush the closed top of the bread thoroughly. Sprinkle the remaining cheese mixture over the top. (You can store the loaf, open-faced at this point in the fridge up to a day, unbaked.)

8. Open loaf, and place on a cookie sheet or directly on the oven rack (with a tray underneath to catch any cheese!). For a room temperature loaf, bake 6 to 9 minutes (or longer depending on how crisp you want it). For a loaf out of the fridge, bake 20 minutes. Then finish it under the broiler for 2 to 3 minutes.

9. Fold it closed, slice into five to six clamshells, and enjoy immediately.

Pro-Tip: Dip the spinach loaf in your favorite red sauce.

"NEVER GO IN AGAINST FRESH SARDINES WHEN PASTA CON SARDE IS ON THE LINE."

That's right, for this dish, it only seems right to commandeer Vizzini's famous line about Sicilians from *The Princess Bride*. The truth is, there are about as many ways to make pasta con sarde (or *pasta con le sarde*) as there are Sicilians in Buffalo. And at least one popular way is to sauté garlic and onions, add tomato paste, then mix in a premade, canned version of the sarde sauce from the store. You toss the pasta in the sauce, garnish with bread crumbs, and *basta! Mangia!*

Unless you have access to a good fish market, the canned version is going to be your best bet most of the year. Italian fish mongers I spoke with said they typically only carry *fresh* sardines the two times a year

that people usually make this dish: for the Feast of St. Joseph and for December's Feast of the Seven Fishes. But (and this is a big but), even as they explained that you can make the dish with the canned sauce, they readily offered that they prefer the sauce made with the fresh sardines! (And it's not like they didn't want to sell the cans.)

It's true, the fresh sauce is a little more work. And you can't be squeamish about handling fish (be sure to ask your fishmonger to clean them for you). But the end result, with the sweetness of the currants, the crunch of the pignolis and bread crumbs . . . no comparison.

PASTA CON SARDE

PREP TIME: 45 minutes ★ **COOKING TIME:** 45 minutes ★ **SERVES:** 6 people

Kosher salt

1 pound fresh sardines, cleaned and deboned

1½ cups panko bread crumbs

1¼ cups olive oil

½ teaspoon saffron

½ cup currants (or golden raisins)

½ cup Pernod

1 cup pine nuts (pignoli)

4 cloves garlic, minced

8 anchovy filets (preferably white marinated anchovies), finely chopped

1 fennel bulb, finely chopped (about 2 cups)

2 medium onions, finely chopped

2 teaspoons capers

2 tablespoons tomato paste

One 14-ounce can crushed tomatoes

½ teaspoon red pepper flakes

Freshly ground black pepper

2 to 3 cups vegetable oil

1 pound perciatelli or bucatini (the long spaghetti tubes)

1½ cups flour

1 cup finely chopped parsley

1. Bring water to a boil in a large pot over high heat, then salt water.

2. Clean and debone sardines, removing heads, tails, skin, and any stray bones. Halve filets and reserve.

3. Preheat oven to 350°F. Scatter bread crumbs over a cookie sheet and drizzle 4 tablespoons olive oil over them, then toast in the oven for 10 minutes. Remove and reserve.

4. Soak saffron in 1 teaspoon warm water and reserve.

5. Soak currants (or golden raisins) in Pernod for 30 minutes to an hour, then strain the liquid (shoot it if you like) and reserve the currants.

6. Warm a saucepan on medium heat, then add pignoli and toast them, tossing frequently for 3 minutes. Remove, combine with bread crumbs, and reserve.

7. Mix garlic with finely chopped anchovies. Reserve.

8. Warm a large saucepan over medium heat. Add ½ cup olive oil. Sauté fennel, onions, currants, and capers until soft, about 3 to 5 minutes. Add garlic-anchovy mixture and tomato paste and cook another 3 minutes. Add crushed tomatoes, red pepper flakes, salt, and pepper, combine, and simmer.

9. Warm a small, deep pot over high heat, then add vegetable oil (enough to submerge the fillets).

10. Cook pasta 8 minutes, then strain and reserve.

continued

11. Meanwhile, lightly toss sardines in the flour until completely coated; then fry sardines in batches, 3 to 4 minutes per batch, flipping filets midway through. (If you have a small fryer, cook 2 to 3 minutes at 380°F.) Remove, then season with salt and pepper.

12. Add a few tablespoons pasta water to sauce, combine, then ladle 1 ½ cups sauce into a large bowl. Reserve a fifth of the bread crumb–pignoli mixture and parsley to use as garnish. Toss the pasta and sauce with the rest of the bread crumb–pignoli mixture and parsley to combine completely.

13. Portion out the pasta and sauce, drizzle 1 tablespoon olive oil over each bowl, and then garnish each with bread crumb–pignoli mixture, parsley, and two to three fried sardine filets.

The Feast of St. Joseph and Pasta con Sarde

In Buffalo, the Feast of St. Joseph is a week observed during Lent when many households and churches prepare meatless dishes, sometimes free for those less fortunate (for the non-Catholics, Lent takes place in the 40 days between Ash Wednesday and Easter Sunday, when Jesus spent time being tempted by Satan in the desert). During this week, a number of Italian restaurants serve set menus featuring some of the most well-known dishes associated with the tradition, like pasta con sarde.

Buffalo's pasta con sarde is made with tomato sauce, fennel, golden raisins, sardines, capers, garlic, and parsley, and then garnished with toasted bread crumbs. The recipe calls for bread crumbs and not grated cheese because cheese was expensive and the crumbs symbolized sacrifice, the poor, and, supposedly, sawdust (Joseph being a carpenter and all). The best versions are made with fresh sardines, and in Sicily, pignoli nuts; but if you look in Guercio & Sons and any other Italian grocer in Buffalo, you'll find premade cans and jars of sarde sauce for sale. If this all sounds dubious tasting, know that when the dish is prepared with fresh ingredients (especially fresh sardines), it's a light, flavorful, non-fishy meal that's at turns salty, sweet, and texturally diverse.

THAT'S HOW BUFFALO (PIZZA) ROLLS

Out-of-towners ask, "Pizza Logs?" But to Buffalonians, these cheesy fried pepperoni sticks are just part of the furniture on appetizer menus in the city's bars and pizzerias. Robert Cordova started his Pizza Logs business in 1992, behind a grocery store in Niagara Falls, where he rolled cheese, pepperoni, and sauce in a crispy wrapper (and it *is* cheese, pepperoni, *and* sauce according to Cordova's son Jason who now runs the company). They're yet another example of why Western New York should get the title "Capital of Finger Foods." Pizza Logs are, however, really nothing like pizza. Imagine a piece of whole milk-mozzarella string cheese turned into a molten center surrounded by about four thin layers of chewy, just-cooked wonton wrapper interwoven with thin slices of pepperoni and wrapped inside a spring roll exterior. Now you get the idea.

There are several handy recipes online. Some suggest you chop up the pepperoni, mix it with cheese and sauce, then roll it all up. That's a messy process. Others suggest mixing in additional ingredients like onions and sausage. While tasty, you have to chop that stuff up pretty fine for it to work. You're better off using those ingredients in a much thicker roll—a pizza egg roll if you will. It's just a heavier snack. I'm a bit of a purist. I like the thinner originals and pretty much stick to cheese, pepperoni, and sauce.

There are a few things to remember while making great logs to make this easy.

★ Use *room temperature* ingredients. Seriously, if the wrappers, cheese, and pepperoni are soft, you'll have a much easier time squishing and rolling them.

★ Use shredded cheese (about ⅓ to ½ unpacked cup per roll). Slices make rolling harder and sticks, while straightforward to roll, mean the cheese isn't as well distributed (you *could* start slicing them lengthwise in thirds, but that starts to get pretty complicated). Neither creates the impressive cheese pull that the shredded cheese does when you bite.

★ If a wrapper tears considerably, and I mean more than a few small little cracks (don't get crazy), toss it, and start over.

★ Last, you *can* bake them—the company makes two versions, one for restaurant fryers and a retail one for the oven—so feel free. But I won't lie: they're better fried.

Pro-Tip: If you want to know how to eat Pizza Logs the way owner Jason Cordova prefers, it's Buffalo style. Cook the logs, let them stand two minutes (so the cheese melts all the way), "and then you brush wing sauce on and then dip it in ranch or blue cheese," Jason told me. "It will change your life."

══════ PIZZA LOGS ══════

PREP TIME: 40 minutes ★ **COOKING TIME:** 12 to 15 minutes
(depending on whether you fry or bake) ★ **YIELD:** 10 rolls

5½ x 5½ egg roll wrappers (start with a full package, or at least twice what you need)

⅓ cup warm water

3⅓ to 5 cups (*unpacked!*) shredded mozzarella

40 slices thin-cut pepperoni

1¼ cups of your favorite jar (or can) tomato sauce

1 tablespoon oregano

Kosher salt

Freshly ground black pepper

1. Preheat oven to 425°F or fryer to 360°F.

2. Lay one egg roll wrapper out flat on the cutting board in front of you so the longest sides form a straight line from your left to right hands (horizontally perpendicular to you).

3. Using the warm water, dip a pastry brush (a finger or the edge of a wet paper towel works just as well) all along the edge of the wrapper so that at least ⅓ inch of the edge of the wrapper is moistened.

4. Evenly scatter ⅓ to ½ cup shredded mozzarella inside the framed area. Leaving about an inch on either side, from one longest diagonal to the other, lay four slices of pepperoni in a line on top of the cheese.

5. Drizzle 1 teaspoon sauce on top of the pepperoni slices, then sprinkle a dash of oregano and salt over the inside of the frame.

continued

6. Starting from the corner nearest you that doesn't start with pepperoni, start softly rolling the tip of the wrapper over on itself and roll it into as thin a tube as you can without rolling so tight that the wrapper tears. Roll until just past the pepperoni at the midway point.

7. Gently fold over the left and right corners as tightly as you reasonably can, then continue rolling the log until you run out of wrapper.

8. Repeat until you complete ten pizza rolls.

9. When ready to serve, warm 1 cup tomato sauce, add salt and pepper to taste, and/or wing sauce over medium heat—for dipping—and serve (with blue cheese or ranch if you plan on testing out Jason's epic advanced move).

10. If using the oven, place rolls on a baking sheet (on a cooling rack if you have one) and bake 12 to 15 minutes, or until golden and delicious. If frying, cook 3 to 6 minutes, then remove. Serve with desired condiments.

IT'S SO EASY BEING CHEESY

Lou Billitier, who started as a dishwasher, working his way through the ranks from busboy to waiter, then restaurant manager, became co-owner of Chef's restaurant in 1950, and took over in 1954. He was the man behind Chef's signature dish, spaghetti Parm, invented over lunch in 1962 with Dave Thomas, the host of a local children's TV show. Supposedly, Billitier added butter and Thomas added the cheese. "Thomas and Billitier were forever 'melted' together by a cold afternoon in '62," the story goes. Lou passed away in 2000, and his son, Lou Jr., runs Chef's now, but "spag Parm" isn't going *anywhere*.

This is apron-wearing food. It comes extra small, small, or large, and arrives like some collapsed, brown-speckled big top from the cheese circus: buttery, broiled to the edges of the dish with a browned edge, and bubbling away, pasta peek-a-booing just barely in a few places, with a cup of sauce on the side for dipping. You twirl the fork, the cheese wraps up with the spaghetti strands as you turn it, you manage the cheese pull, dip into the side of sauce, and *mangia*! After you've twirled through it and gotten your guaranteed cheese pulls, there's that magic orange melted-cheese, butter, and sauce shimmer.

The recipe is simple. Still, stick to the rules to get the full effect, which means slices of mozzarella, not the shredded stuff. You get better coverage that way. A few notes: Meatballs and sausages make a great accompaniment (when don't they?), but they aren't *required*. If you dig those, have at it using your favorite recipes. Next, Chef's sauce, like most Buffalo tomato sauces, is sweet. If you want to achieve the authentic effect, add a teaspoon of sugar and a half-cup of red wine to your sauce as you warm and then reduce it.

As much as it may seem indulgent, I offer one tweak to the original recipe if I may be so bold. Even with so much cheese draped over the top, once you twirl into it, it disappears faster than you'd think. As a solution to this problem, I suggest thoroughly lining the bottom of the bowl with a single layer of room temperature mozzarella slices before piling the pasta in. It'll start melting with the heat of the pasta and continue in the oven under the broiler.

You may even consider portioning individual servings in separate bowls before broiling, each lined with mozzarella! Trust me. You (and your guests) will be thankful.

SPAGHETTI PARM
═══ (MEATBALLS AND SAUSAGE NOT INCLUDED) ═══

PREP TIME: 15 minutes ★ **COOKING TIME:** 30 minutes ★ **SERVES:** 4 people

2 teaspoons kosher salt

1 jar Chef's tomato sauce (or your favorite store-bought sauce!)

1 teaspoon sugar (optional)

½ cup red wine (optional)

1 pound spaghetti

5 tablespoons butter

2 packages (about 21 slices) thinly sliced mozzarella

1. Bring water to a boil in a large pot over high heat, then salt water.

continued

2. Pour a jar of your favorite spaghetti sauce in a small saucepan and bring to a simmer. Optional: add a teaspoon of sugar and a half-cup of red wine.

3. When the water boils, add spaghetti and stir occasionally for 8 minutes until al dente, then strain and toss into a large bowl.

4. Add butter and about 8 ounces sauce to spaghetti and toss until butter is completely melted and sauce is combined thoroughly.

5. Make sure the top shelf in your oven is at the highest rung, then turn your broiler on high.

6. Line the bottom of a large, oven-safe bowl with a single layer of cheese using up to eight slices. Cover with butter-and-sauce-tossed spaghetti.

7. Using about 13 slices of mozzarella, top bowl of spaghetti to completely cover it.

8. Carefully place bowl directly under the broiler and leave it for about 3 to 5 minutes.

9. Remove and serve with a side of sauce, instructing your guests to mind the bowl. "It's hot!"

STINGS SO GOOD

As any growing Buffalo boy or girl knows, the "stinger" is a combination of steak and chicken fingers, usually joined in hoagie matrimony, but also turned into pizza, burritos, and yes, tacos. There are several around town likely worthy of your attention, but the one that came up repeatedly during my search was one at Colosso Taco & Subs in Tonawanda. And it has been the obsession of 35-year-old chef and Buffalo native son Ed Forster since high school. He told me that for him, the stinger taco is just a great mix of nostalgia, comfort food, and "that inner desire to be a fat kid."

Forster says there's nothing, ahem, farm-to-table about its components. The reason he's obsessed is its texture and flavor contrast: "You have spicy and super acidic Frank's, which is huge here in Buffalo, and you juxtapose it with the salt, fattiness, and creaminess of blue cheese; the salty, seared, chopped steak; and crispy-on-the-outside, meaty chicken tenders."

You may be closer to the original if you load your cart with frozen and prepared foods, but if you make it from scratch, whomever you cook for will never look at you the same again. Store-bought tortillas, however, are sanctioned. Ed says he only ever orders the large taco, but that version feels to me like it's auditioning for a role of leading burrito. I suggest going with two smaller tortillas per person. I know this sounds crazy, but if you *really* want to geek out, they're easily replaced by homemade ones.

I riff on Diana Barrios Treviño's recipe (she runs a bunch of great Tex-Mex restaurants in San Antonio, Texas). All you have to do is mix the flour, salt, baking powder, shortening, butter (the *flavor* of butter tortillas is addicting), and water, divide the

dough in eight round balls (*testales*), then roll each out and griddle. You'll have twice more than what you'll need but you can layer them between parchment and freeze them before griddling to use for a later date.

Ask your butcher for some ribeye shaved thinly on the slicer (raw, obviously), then grab some chicken tenderloins. You can use breasts, but Ed advises you make them torpedo-shaped for "better balance." We're talking an inch square by four inches long. When they cook they should be no more than a half-inch thick. The steak should be barely cooked on low heat and uncaramelized. And the order?

"Tortilla, cheese, lettuce, tomato, and a thin layer of onion," Forster explains. "Then the two chicken tenders kind of yin-yanged in, so you have a meeting point in the middle which is a little thicker with chicken. And that's where you put the two ends of the breasts, the two tails, towards the waistline. Then just cover that in steak meat, and cover your steak with blue cheese."

BUFFALO STINGER TACO

PREP TIME: 25 to 40 minutes (the latter if making tortillas) ★ **COOKING TIME:** 18 to 42 minutes (the latter if making tortillas) ★ **YIELD:** 2 to 4 tacos

TORTILLAS

1¼ cups flour

½ teaspoon kosher salt, plus more for seasoning

¼ teaspoon baking powder

1½ tablespoons vegetable shortening

1½ tablespoons butter, room temperature

¼ cup warm water

Alternative: Four 8-inch or four 6-inch store-bought flour tortillas

FILLING

4 cups shredded iceberg lettuce

2 large tomatoes, cut in small cubes

1 large white onion, cut in small cubes

⅓ cup flour

1 egg, beaten

½ cup bread crumbs (or Buffalo Bread Crumbs, page 98)

6 to 8 boneless, skinless chicken breast tenderloins

One 16-ounce ribeye steak, thinly sliced

Freshly ground black pepper

2 tablespoons butter

4 to 8 slices provolone (1 each for small tortillas, 2 for large)

1 cup Buffalo Wing Sauce (page 22)

1 cup Homemade Blue Cheese Dressing (page 38)

1. Make the tortillas: Mix flour, ½ teaspoon salt, and baking powder in a large bowl. Add shortening, butter, and warm water, mixing until a soft dough forms. Divide into eight small balls and roll them out with a rolling pin on a well-floured surface to form 6-inch-wide tortillas.

2. Warm a skillet or saucepan over medium heat. When hot, cook tortillas one at a time over low, 2 minutes on the first side (until a few brown spots form), 1 minute on the second. Repeat until finished. Alternatively, use four 8-inch or four 6-inch store-bought flour tortillas.

3. Make the filling: Preheat fryer (or fryer oil in a skillet) to 350°F.

4. Stack a pile of six to eight lettuce leaves, roll them up, and finely slice to shred. Reserve.

5. Cut tomatoes and onions in cubes about the same size.

6. Set up a dredge station using three containers long enough to hold the chicken fingers: flour, egg, and bread crumbs.

7. Evenly coat chicken fingers on all sides first in flour, then egg, then bread crumbs.

8. Season ribeye on both sides with salt and pepper. Set a skillet on low heat and add butter. When it melts, add steak. Cook 2 to 3 minutes on each side.

continued

9. Meanwhile, carefully release half the chicken fingers into the oil. Cook 4 to 5 minutes, then remove to a drying rack or paper towels. Repeat.

10. Steam tortillas if using store-bought. If using a microwave, wet two paper towels. Place tortilla on one wet towel, line the center of the tortilla with cheese, and place a second paper towel over the top, tenting it over the cheese so it won't stick. You should have enough room to be able to do two at a time. Nuke 20 to 35 seconds.

11. Cover the cheese in the center of the tortilla first with lettuce, then tomatoes, then onions.

12. Toss tenders in ⅓ cup wing sauce to completely cover. Layer fingers on top of onions (two per small taco, four per large taco).

13. Layer steak on top (4 ounces per small tacos, 8 ounces on large ones).

14. Drizzle Blue Cheese Dressing over the top of each taco (about 2 tablespoons per small taco, 3 tablespoons per large taco).

15. Serve with remaining Blue Cheese Dressing and Buffalo Wing Sauce for dipping.

A PEPPER RECIPE BUFFALO'S GONE BANANAS FOR

The original recipe for cheese-stuffed Hungarian peppers is credited to Andy DiVincenzo. He created the dish for the Taste of Buffalo festival in the summer of 1990, and served them at his restaurant Billy Ogden's until he died in 2004. Billy Ogden's lasted just a few years without Andy, but his dish has taken on a life of its own.

Christopher Daigler, chef and owner of Buffalo restaurant Falley Allen, who worked for DiVincenzo and cooked the peppers at his side, told *Buffalo Spree* that only Andy and Andy's grandmother had the real recipe. But today, you can find many versions—if not everywhere, enough places that you don't have to go looking. They've even become ingredients that routinely top other dishes, namely pizzas and subs.

This recipe is based on techniques Daigler learned while working with DiVincenzo, and with ingredients pulled together while inventing a refreshed stuffed pepper recipe for *Buffalo Spree*. Stuffed banana peppers are known as a spicy dish, but the kind of peppers you choose should determine *how* spicy. Banana peppers and Hungarian wax peppers are pretty similar, usually running between four and six inches long. But whereas banana peppers typically run zero to 500 Scoville units, Hungarian wax peppers can range from 1,000 to 15,000 (jalapeños run 2,500 to 5,000), giving you a little more oomph. Consider playing stuffed pepper roulette, and use one Hungarian wax pepper!

You can take creative license with the stuffing, keeping a few things in mind. You're going to want cream cheese or ricotta as a thick base cheese so that it doesn't all seep out during the cooking. From there, feel free to add to that stringy cheese pull effect with shredded Cheddar, mozzarella, Swiss, Gruyère, Jack, Fontal, Emmental, or Muenster. And flavor them with a distinctive cheese like crumbled blue, Gorgonzola, Parmesan, Asiago, Romano, or even goat cheese. But you'll want at least one cheese from each of those three groups!

There are a few simple but key things to remember. You need to prep the peppers at least one hour ahead of cooking time because they need to firm up in the fridge. Consider cooking them in a mix of olive and either vegetable, peanut, or safflower oil (the olive oil for flavor, the other oil for a higher smoke point). Just be careful when you put the peppers in: They're going to spit and ooze! Usually the peppers are served with slices of Italian bread, for dipping in the oil and cheese, or toasted, as a conveyance method. A side of sauce is optional. And lastly, the peppers can be sliced in rounds when they're removed from the fridge, fried in a pan about a minute on each side, and then used as toppings for sandwiches, pasta, or just as a side! Buffalo food writer Christa Glennie Seychew notes that the leftovers (as *if*) are great mixed in the next morning with scrambled eggs.

STUFFED BANANA PEPPERS

PREP TIME: 80 minutes ★ **COOKING TIME:** 15 minutes ★ **YIELD:** 5 peppers

10 banana peppers

1½ cups cream cheese

1 cup crumbled Gorgonzola

1 cup mascarpone

1 cup shredded mozzarella

½ cup grated Parmesan

½ cup grated Romano

2 teaspoons ground white pepper

1 tablespoon anchovy paste

4 tablespoons chopped parsley

¼ teaspoon kosher salt

½ cup Italian bread crumbs

1 cup of your favorite spaghetti sauce or crushed tomatoes (optional)

¼ cup canola-olive oil blend

4 tablespoons chopped garlic

Fresh Italian bread, sliced

1. Cut off pepper stem ends (reserve them and fry them with the peppers if you like) and, keeping the peppers as completely intact as possible, remove the seeds and ribs.

2. Make stuffing: Combine cheeses, white pepper, anchovy paste, 2 tablespoons chopped parsley, and salt. Mix completely, then gently fold in bread crumbs until filling thickens.

3. Put stuffing in one corner of a large Ziploc bag, cut off the corner, and gently pipe stuffing into the peppers until completely full. Refrigerate for an hour (or more).

4. Remove peppers from fridge.

5. If using, pour your favorite spaghetti sauce (or crushed tomatoes) in a small saucepan and bring to a simmer.

6. Heat a large skillet on high. Add oil blend. Once oil begins to smoke, add peppers and sear on both sides, about 2 to 3 minutes each. Place peppers on serving plate (or two plates).

7. Add garlic to remaining oil in the hot pan and brown 1 minute. Add remaining 2 tablespoons parsley and toss; then pour oil, garlic, and parsley mixture over peppers.

8. Optional: Serve with a side of sauce or drizzle sauce under and/or over the top of the peppers.

9. Serve with sliced Italian bread for sopping up any cheese, sauce, or garlic mixture you may have missed.

HOT DIGGITY!

Theodore Spiro Liaros came from Greece to Buffalo in 1912, and started on his path to the American dream by selling popcorn and peanuts from a box around his neck. He started a lunch wagon and when the Peace Bridge (built to connect with Canada over Lake Erie) was completed in 1927, he bought a construction shack nearby and started selling hot dogs cooked on a flat grill. In 1948, he opened Ted's on Shirley Drive, and soon after Ted's son suggested they cook over charcoal. "Somewhere around 1950, they switched," Ted's president (and Theodore's granddaughter) Thecly Liaros Ortolani

told me. "And it's ironic, because that's what differentiates us now, everything cooked over charcoal."

The original Ted's closed in 1969, but the tradition continues, complete with Theodore's "Famous Hot Chili Sauce," a secret recipe. For the uninitiated, this isn't the chili for a chili dog, or the meat sauce typical to Greek hot dogs or Coney dogs, but a sweet-spicy, ketchup-based condiment.

Thecly says her grandfather's recipe is locked in a safe like the original formula for Coca-Cola. He supposedly brought it with him *from* Greece in 1912, and passed it down to his sons, Spiro and

Peter. In 1905, Heinz was selling five million bottles of ketchup, so it's possible the original recipe *did* use ketchup. There's *also* folklore that one of Liaros's vendors had a wife who made it. Either way, the ingredients are listed on the bottle (sold online), Thecly confirmed there's ketchup in it, and it *is* fun to try to replicate.

While this recipe might not be a dead ringer, it comes close enough and tastes good regardless. You can keep what you don't use in the fridge for a few weeks, if there's any left. If you're going to be authentic, order Sahlen's hot dogs online in advance. At Ted's, they shoot for 15 minutes over charcoal, during which the dogs are blackened, poked (to control where the split happens and to keep the dogs straight, so you can roll them), coddled, and turned until they're browned in most places.

TED'S HOT DOG RELISH

PREP TIME: 8 minutes ★ **COOKING TIME:** 8 minutes ★ **YIELD:** 2¾ cups

2 tablespoons vegetable oil

½ medium white onion, diced

½ red bell pepper, cleaned and diced

2 cups ketchup

½ cup white wine vinegar

3 tablespoons crushed red hot pepper relish

2 tablespoons sweet relish

¼ cup Worcestershire sauce

¼ cup soy sauce

1 tablespoon onion powder

1 tablespoon garlic powder

½ teaspoon anchovy paste

1. Heat a large saucepan over a medium flame. Add vegetable oil and, when it's hot, the onion and pepper. Cook until soft (about 3 minutes).

2. Add all remaining ingredients, stir well, and bring to a boil. Remove from heat, let cool, then drape all over your hot dogs.

SPONGE CANDY CAPITAL OF THE WORLD

Cinder toffee, golden crunchers, seafoam—you may have heard one of these words *if* you visit candy stores when you travel, but they're just as likely to be as unfamiliar to you as to folks from along Lake Erie's eastern shore, where there's one name for this love-it-or-hate-it confection. And while other places may be outposts in this "Sponge Candy Crescent," Buffalonians, even those in the hate-it camp, will agree with former *Buffalo News* restaurant critic Janice Okun, who says there's no doubt that "Buffalo is the sponge candy capital of the world."

Sponge candy has been described by those who love it as a light, crunchy, delicate toffee, or a fluffy meringue crossed with a milk ball. But it's a contrast in appearance versus reality. You think the chocolate covering will disappear as you crunch into the center, but the opposite happens! The center is sandy enough to blow away and it leaves behind a chocolate finish.

Like beef on weck, this candy's history intersects with the Pan-Am Exposition in 1901 (in some stories), where Joe Fowler, an English immigrant, was said to have been successful enough selling confections to inspire opening a store. Fowler supposedly introduced Buffalo to the candy he learned to make in England. According to Western New York's regional magazine, *Buffalo Spree*, other stories attribute the creation to a mistake in New England. Either way, it's been said that, like oysters, sponge candy can only be eaten in months that end in 'r.' At least, it's very sensitive to heat and humidity. When it's been exposed to those, the center collapses into a gum. Some confectioners, like Ko-Ed, which closes for the summer, contend that the season makes keeping it untenable. They just won't make it.

But *you* can. You just need a candy thermometer. Sugar, corn syrup, and baking soda are the ingredients frequently cited, with some recipes calling for vinegar or gelatin to stabilize the bubbles. Baking soda causes the carbon dioxide to bubble and get caught in the mixture. Then it's cooled and the candy is dipped in dark chocolate, milk chocolate, or orange-infused chocolate. If that sounds anodyne, watch a video of it being made. It can seem more like the forging of one ring to rule them all. Just remember, it won't keep much longer than a week in an airtight container.

If you're the type who gets a shiver from scraping ice or scratching nails on a chalkboard, maybe leave cutting sponge candy to someone else. Slicing into those hardened sugar bubbles can be cringe-inducing. And try as you might, you'll be

lucky if the cuts are even. Expect shards, dust, and jagged edges. Turns out, sponge candy is like snowflakes: no two pieces made this way will be alike. Silicone ice cube trays can help with uniform shapes, but it can be messy. Embrace the chaos.

Here's a thought for when you get tired after dipping the twentieth piece: lay the remaining pieces on a parchment-lined tray and drizzle the chocolate over them instead of going for full coverage. (If you do that, you also only need half the chocolate.)

SPONGE CANDY

PREP TIME: 3 hours (1 hour active) ★ **COOKING TIME:** 25 minutes ★ **YIELD:** About 40 pieces

4 tablespoons butter

¼ teaspoon powdered gelatin

1 tablespoon water

1 cup sugar

½ teaspoon sea salt

1 cup dark corn syrup

1 tablespoon vinegar

1 tablespoon baking soda, sifted

16 ounces milk (or semisweet) chocolate

1. Line a 9-inch square pan with 2 tablespoons butter. Then line pan with parchment paper to cover the bottom and sides. Grease paper with butter.

2. Use a measuring cup to bloom gelatin in water.

3. In a large pot with high sides, combine sugar, salt, corn syrup, and vinegar over medium heat, stirring until sugar dissolves.

4. Cook until thermometer reads 300°F (about 10 to 15 minutes). Turn off heat. Wait 1 minute for bubbling to subside, then quickly whisk in gelatin.

5. Keep a spatula handy and prepare for the mixture to bubble after this next step. Sprinkle baking soda over syrup and whisk

vigorously. The mixture will bubble with equal energy.

6. Pour into center of lined pan, using the spatula to guide it and get as much out as you can.

7. Don't worry about spreading the mixture out. Just let it settle, cool, and set at least 2 hours (or overnight).

8. When completely cool, use the paper to lift the hardened candy out of the pan. Use a serrated knife to score lines in the candy, creating inch-square candies.

9. Slice or break apart along score lines (you can save shards to use as ice cream topping).

10. Use a double-boiler to melt chocolate. Lay out a Silpat or parchment paper. Use either a fork or tongs to dip candy into chocolate, cover on all sides, then place on paper to set chocolate. If you like, use a toothpick to sign your initials or create some other symbol on the top of the still warm chocolate à la Buffalo's famed sponge candy shop Alethea's.

THE BEST HOLIDAY COCKTAIL RECIPE YOU'VE NEVER HAD

If Christmas was a dessert, this would be what it tasted like. A creamy sweetness fills the mouth, your throat and belly warm up, and the healthy dose of rum and brandy does something to your brain that makes you squint with happiness. What is it? Not eggnog. At least, not the supermarket 'nog you buy during the Thanksgiving and Christmas holidays.

Eggnog, by definition, consists of eggs beaten with sugar, milk or cream, and often, liquor. The Tom & Jerry is light, airy, and topped with a thick, sweet, egg-white cloud that hot water or milk rises to its top. Both use yolks and whites whipped with sugar. Eggnog *sometimes* gets booze while a Tom & Jerry always does. And eggnog *always* gets milk or cream, but a Tom & Jerry only *sometimes* does. A Tom & Jerry doesn't get warmed over the stove like eggnog often does, and doesn't get the air whisked out like eggnog does. One last difference may be because Tom & Jerrys are made for customers who expect enough rosy-cheeked liquid courage to make for memorable holiday parties: Unlike most recipes for uncooked eggnogs, which typically call for booze to be incorporated *before* the whipped-to-peaks egg whites are folded in, Tom & Jerrys at Buffalo's best spots for them get brandy and rum added after.

As Jason McCarthy, co-owner of The Place (Buffalo's most famous spot for a Tom & Jerry) says, "Hot water to warm the cup. Then your batter, then your booze. Then you put hot water on *top* of the batter so it fluffs it and it pushes it up to the top. A little sprinkle of nutmeg and then you serve it and give them a spoon."

Buffalo didn't invent the Tom & Jerry. Neither did any of the cities near the Great Lakes, where it's also popular. But it really is a big thing in the Nickel City (where you can find it from Black Friday up to a few days before the end of the year), and sipping one takes you back in time. Two gentlemen are usually credited for its creation. Some say the best-selling nineteenth-century British writer Pierce Egan invented it as a publicity move for one of his books, naming it for two central characters in *Life in London or, The Day and Night Scenes of Jerry Hawthorn, Esq., and his Elegant Friend Corinthian Tom in Their Rambles and Sprees Through the Metropolis.* And as the other story goes, Jerry Thomas, the legendary New York barman of the 1800s, claimed to have invented it. But in his book, *Imbibe!,* David Wondrich dismantles Jerry's claims, citing an 1827 article mentioning the drink (Thomas was born in 1830), but adds that Jerry did more than any other man to promote it.

TOM & JERRY COCKTAIL

PREP TIME: 18 minutes (and about 1 to 2 minutes per cocktail) ★ **YIELD:** 12 to 18 drinks

1 dozen eggs, separated

½ cup granulated sugar

¼ teaspoon kosher salt

2 dashes Angostura bitters

2 teaspoons vanilla extract

2 teaspoons cinnamon

1 teaspoon allspice

½ teaspoon nutmeg

1 kettle boiling water

1 teaspoon cream of tartar

1 cup powdered sugar

FOR EACH COCKTAIL:

1 ounce añejo rum

1 ounce VS Cognac

6 ounces hot water (whole milk, coffee, or a
    mix of the two can also be used)

Nutmeg, for garnish

1. Separate eggs.

2. Beat yolks until thoroughly mixed.
Add sugar, salt, bitters, vanilla, cinnamon,
allspice, and nutmeg and whisk until
completely combined.

3. Pour boiled water into first batch of mugs.

4. If you have one, use a stand mixer or
hand mixer for beating the whites to stiff
peaks (make sure the bowl is clean and
dry). If you don't have a mixer, prepare for
a forearm workout. Add cream of tartar to
whites *before* beating, then gradually add
powdered sugar as you whisk. Continue
beating the whites until stiff peaks form
(about 5 minutes).

5. Empty the first mug, discarding the water.
Add booze, then spoon in 3 tablespoons
batter. Pour in hot water (sub milk, coffee,
or milk-coffee mix here), stir slightly, add
more batter if necessary, and garnish with a
sprinkle of nutmeg.

6. Repeat until you run out of batter or
there's nobody left standing.

Note: You'll never see a bartender remove
batter from the fridge in between making
cocktails. It's typically left on or behind the
bar in a large punch bowl and ladled out
of as needed. But as the warning goes,
consuming raw or undercooked eggs may
increase your risk of foodborne illness. If
you're *really* worried, the warning doesn't
apply to pasteurized eggs, which you can buy
from a company called Davidson's Safest
Choice Eggs.

SHREDDED BUFFALO CHICKEN (PAGE 101)

BUFFALO "BASICS"

◆———◆———◆

Wing sauce, blue cheese dressing—sure, these are the core recipes to Buffalo "flavor," but we've covered those elsewhere. Here, in addition, are a few quick and relatively easy recipes that carry those flavors and impart their spirit into a few other components that can be eaten on their own (Buffalo bacon), deployed as toppings (blue cheese sour cream) or breading (Buffalo bread crumbs), and used as vehicles to carry Buffalo flavor through every dish imaginable in your personal comfort food vocabulary (shredded Buffalo chicken).

SOUR CREAM . . . PLUS

This basic recipe adds panache to almost everything sour cream normally ornaments. You can use it to top baked potatoes, nachos, potato pancakes, scrambled eggs, and pierogi, or mix it into potato salad, mashed potatoes, and biscuits, or add horseradish to it for topping steak, or throw in some diced onions for a potato chip dip. I'm not convinced that blue cheese sour cream made with milder blues wouldn't work in cakes (cheesecake, upside-down, coffee) and even icings paired with certain cakes too.

Making different dips with this recipe by mixing various types of blue cheese in sour cream can make for some very happy guests. But blue cheese can be particularly powerful and the range of softness can make some more difficult to seamlessly blend. Soft, mild, sweet, and slightly funky blues work really well. The go-to in most of this book is a cow's milk cheese from central France called Saint Agur Blue. It's a pasteurized, double-cream cheese that's tangy, a little sweet, not too salty, and easily spreadable. But you can't go wrong with Italian Gorgonzola Dolce or Bleu d'Auvergne from south central France either.

BLUE CHEESE SOUR CREAM

PREP TIME: 5 to 10 minutes ★ **YIELD:** 1 cup

½ **pound Saint Agur Blue**

½ **cup sour cream**

¼ **cup milk**

1. If you prefer chunks of blue in the sour cream, mix the cheese and sour cream with a spoon in a bowl by hand. For a

continued

smooth, thoroughly blended sour cream, mix in a food processor or blender for 1 to 2 minutes, adding a little milk to thin it to your preferred consistency. My personal winner? A bit of both: well-incorporated with the occasional soft blue cheese nugget. Reserve a third of the cheese and stir it in after incorporating the rest.

Buffalo All the Way: Add ¼ cup Frank's RedHot Sauce and ½ cup minced celery for an easy Buffalo-ized dip.

Homemade Buffalo Blue Cheese Onion Dip: Sauté 1½ cups diced onions in olive oil with kosher salt over medium heat 20 minutes (until caramelized) and mix into blue cheese sour cream with ½ cup mayonnaise, and pinches of white pepper and garlic powder.

BUFFALO SAUCE + BACON = NO-BRAINER

This is not reinventing the wheel here, and the directions are basically "brush bacon with Buffalo sauce on both sides and bake," but it makes sense on *so* many levels. Bacon is already awesome, but coating it with butter? Ridiculously over-the-top but also, um, yeah!? Next, making

this recipe is basically as easy as how you might normally cook bacon for a big hungry crowd (in the oven), but it adds a little extra zip to your favorite breakfast classics. It's just so damn good. And you also have Buffalo bacon bits for salad, and, well, anything?

A third of a cup of Buffalo sauce is enough for nine slices, but heck, if you want to double up on the sauce, or even lose the baking tray and just lay the bacon on the foil in all that excess buttery wing sauce and rendered bacon grease, whoever you're cooking for is not going to complain. Not unless they're wimps or health-nuts, at least. And if they are, why're you cooking for them, anyway? (Just plan on cooking it for 12 to 20 minutes and start checking around the 10-minute mark.)

BUFFALO-IZED BACON

PREP TIME: 10 minutes ★ **COOKING TIME:** 20 to 30 minutes ★ **YIELD:** 9 slices

9 bacon slices
⅓ cup Buffalo Wing Sauce (page 22)

1. Preheat oven to 400°F.

2. Line a cookie tray with foil and set a baking rack in the tray.

3. Lay out bacon evenly on the rack.

4. Brush each slice with Buffalo Wing Sauce, flip, and repeat.

5. Slide bacon into the oven and set a timer for 20 minutes.

6. Check bacon and cook another 5 to 10 minutes (or to desired crispiness), then serve!

ALL THE FLAVOR, NONE OF THE MESS

In my book, any way you can overcomplicate, er . . . riff on the elements of Buffalo's signature dish *within* one component demands respect. And when you can do it easily . . . well, that's a bonus. There's no butter in this recipe (and nothing will ever measure up to slathering on sauce) but by adding vinegar and cayenne powders to store-bought (or homemade) bread crumbs, you'll add a tangy heat reminiscent of that iconic flavor to whatever you're using them for, be it breading chicken fingers, in an oreganata, as a zippy crust for mac and cheese, or as a finishing touch for pastas, salads, or gratins.

Here's another tip: forget the bread crumbs altogether. Go ahead and use the seasoning to toss on popcorn or potato chips.

BUFFALO BREAD CRUMBS

PREP TIME: 5 minutes ★ **YIELD:** 1½ cups bread crumbs

1 cup bread crumbs

4 tablespoons vinegar powder

2 teaspoons onion powder

2 teaspoons garlic powder

2 teaspoons cayenne powder

½ teaspoon freshly ground black pepper

1 teaspoon kosher salt

1. Mix all ingredients and adjust seasoning.

バッファローウィングパン粉

It's hard to believe that *panko* (Japanese for "bread crumbs") were something you had to go to a specialty store for at the turn of the century. Panko's large, light, airy flakes are made from white bread and are said to absorb less oil, making them crunchier than your run-of-the-mill crumbs.

These days, you can find panko at most major supermarkets. They're handy for adding extra texture to fried foods, and responsible for the signature crunch and appearance of chicken katsu. These are slightly more of a pain to make than Buffalo bread crumbs (and by soaking them in butter then toasting them, you do sacrifice a little of that original crunch), but if you're *really* looking to impart instantly recognizable wing sauce flavor (butter factor included), it's the way to go.

If a recipe calls for fine bread crumbs, you can use the Buffalo bread crumb recipe. But if you want that classic buttery wing sauce flavor, consider pulsing these in a food processor or blender for 1 minute after letting them cool.

BUFFALO PANKO

PREP TIME: 5 minutes ★ **COOKING TIME:** 1 hour and 2 minutes ★

YIELD: 1 cup bread crumbs

1 cup panko bread crumbs

½ cup Buffalo Wing Sauce (page 22)

1. Preheat oven to 350°F.

2. Line a cookie sheet with parchment paper (or a Silpat). Lightly brush the surface with Buffalo Wing Sauce.

3. In a large bowl, toss bread crumbs in Buffalo Wing Sauce until evenly coated.

4. Spread bread crumbs out on a large tray as evenly as possible, spreading out clumps. You can top them with another layer of parchment and flatten them with another pan (just don't smash them).

5. Bake 1 hour, stirring and tossing every 15 minutes. Remove, cool, crumble any clumps, and reserve.

WHERE THE BUFFALO REFRIED BEANS ROAM

Doubtless, *some* Lone State denizens may balk at the idea that a central component in Tex-Mex cuisine, refried beans, could use any improvement. After all, they make a great dip, they're essential for breakfast tacos and tostadas, and no combo plate is complete without them. But if it's completely legit to make refried beans doctored with jalapeños (it is), why not a Buffalo riff? Turns out they carry the flavor of hot sauce and butter *really* well, which shouldn't be a surprise considering most legit recipes call for fat, usually in the form of lard or bacon grease, and the vinegary heat adds a welcome tang to accent the silkiness of the beans. Like straight-up refried beans, this Buffalo-ized version is addictive scooped up on chips, but it's also great with shredded or roasted Buffalo chicken eaten on nachos, tacos, Mexican "pizzas," 7-layer dip, and any other way you could use a little.

BUFFALO REFRIED BEANS

PREP TIME: 10 minutes ★ **COOKING TIME:** 1 hour and 45 minutes (15 active) ★ **YIELD:** 3 cups

1½ cups dry pinto beans

1 teaspoon kosher salt

¼ cup lard

1 onion, chopped

4 cloves garlic, minced

One 4-ounce can pickled chiles or jalapeños, finely chopped

½ teaspoon cayenne

¼ teaspoon freshly ground black pepper

½ teaspoon cumin

½ cup Buffalo Wing Sauce (page 22)

1. In a large pot, cover pinto beans with 5 cups water and salt. Boil, then simmer 90 minutes, and cool.

2. Purée half of the beans and water in a blender or food processor for 2 minutes. Repeat with second half.

3. Warm the emptied large pot again over medium heat. Add lard. When it melts, add onion and cook 2 minutes. Add garlic, cook 2 more minutes. Add pickled chiles (and juice) and cook 2 more minutes.

4. Add puréed beans, cayenne, black pepper, cumin, and Buffalo Wing Sauce. Stir to thoroughly combine, cook 5 minutes, then serve.

BRING OUT THE (HOMEMADE) BEST

I don't know about you, but it's hard to believe the part of an origin story that involves a frazzled mother making homemade mayo while trying to throw together a meal for her son and his hungry friends when they bum-rushed her bar on a Friday night. No doubt, Teressa Bellissimo reached for Hellman's, Duke's, or Miracle Whip. But if you're going to go to the trouble of making your own blue cheese dressing, it's hard to imagine anything contributing to a better one than homemade mayo. You'll find it tends to be creamier and have a little more of a pleasant tang.

═ HOMEMADE MAYONNAISE (AND BUFFALO MAYO) ═

PREP TIME: 10 minutes ★ **YIELD:** 1 cup

1 egg yolk
½ teaspoon dry tin mustard
½ teaspoon kosher salt
Freshly ground black pepper
½ teaspoon Dijon mustard
2 teaspoons white vinegar
1 teaspoon lemon juice
1 cup vegetable or olive oil (or a combination)

1. Place yolk in a mixing bowl, add dry mustard, and salt and pepper to taste.

2. In a separate bowl, combine wet mustard, vinegar, and lemon juice. Add half yolk mixture and beat vigorously with a wire whisk.

3. Add oil gradually (just drops at a time over 10 seconds!), beating continuously with the whisk. When the mixture starts to thicken, ridge, and swirl, you can relax, gradually adding oil at a quicker pace, while whisking in until all is used.

Just Add Franks: Adding ¼ cup Frank's RedHot Sauce to homemade mayonnaise makes ketchup and mustard an afterthought for dipping fries.

GET SHREDDED

You can use this recipe as the main event sandwiched into warmed hamburger buns with just blue cheese dressing, or on a hoagie roll with blue cheese dressing, provolone, celery shavings, shredded lettuce, and slices of tomato. And it's similarly great on slider rolls as a party starter.

It's been paired with both real pasta (Buffal-fredo, lasagna, baked ziti) and spaghetti squash, served in quinoa bowls and with rice, nestled into lettuce wraps, and turned into more clever appetizers and entrées than you could really even begin to count: quesadillas, zucchini boats, loaded celery sticks, wonton cups, rangoons, egg rolls, stuffed peppers, twice-baked sweet potatoes, and loaded French fries among them. In fact, it's one of several basic recipes routinely used in *other* recipes in this book (nachos, twice-baked potatoes, biscuit bombs, cheesy chicken ring, grilled cheese, pimento salad), and something that could be subbed into others for the chicken breast that's been called for.

Of course, the easiest thing to do would be to buy a rotisserie chicken, discard the skin, and shred away. You get about 3 cups of meat from the average rotisserie chicken; figure on one to two batches of wing sauce per 3 cups. But if you're going from scratch, you can bake, poach (in the oven or on the stovetop), or slow-cook (though the poached and slow-cooked versions feel like they absorb the most flavor). Speaking of which, if you're going to poach your chicken, don't poach it in water and then douse it in sauce. Just skip the water or stock step and go ahead and poach in the sauce! And while you can go with straight-

up chicken breasts, consider going half boneless, skinless breasts and half thighs to add a little more richness to the meat. (Swap thighs out of any of the following shredded chicken recipes for an additional two breasts.)

If you're a devotee of the Instant Pot, the multi-use pressure cooker, you'll probably guess that it's the quickest way to go, but here are four easy techniques depending on the time or equipment you have.

One-Up: Consider adding ½ cup minced celery and $^1/_3$ cup blue cheese dressing for an easy dip (or blue cheese just to mellow out the sauce and make the chicken creamier); tricking out with sriracha or your favorite hot peppers (fresh or pickled, and diced); tossing with cream cheese and your favorite shredded cheese for a dip; or finishing with a drizzle of honey (1 teaspoon) for topping toast or French bread pizza.

SHREDDED BUFFALO CHICKEN (INSTANT POT)

PREP TIME: 5 minutes ★ **COOKING TIME:** 15 minutes ★ **YIELD:** 4 to 5 cups

2 boneless, skinless chicken breasts
5 boneless, skinless chicken thighs
Kosher salt
Freshly ground black pepper
2 cups Buffalo Wing Sauce (page 22)

1. Season chicken on all sides with salt and pepper. Pile into the bottom of Instant Pot, making as even a layer as possible. Pour Buffalo Wing Sauce over top of chicken. Cover and secure lid.

2. Cook on the "Manual" high pressure setting for 10 minutes.

3. When time's up, turn the valve to allow pressure to release on its own.

4. Remove chicken to a bowl or tray and rest 15 minutes. Meanwhile, turn Instant Pot's Sauté setting on and reduce liquid by about a third.

5. Shred chicken with two forks or pull apart with your fingers.

6. Toss with reduced sauce.

Whoa, Buffalo: For plain Instant Pot shredded chicken, add ¼ cup olive oil and 2 cups chicken stock.

— SHREDDED BUFFALO CHICKEN (OVEN-ROASTED) —

PREP TIME: 30 minutes (about 15 active) ★
COOKING TIME: 30 to 35 minutes ★ **YIELD:** 4 to 5 cups

2 boneless, skinless chicken breasts
5 boneless, skinless chicken thighs
2 cups Buffalo Wing Sauce (page 22)
Kosher salt
Freshly ground black pepper

1. Preheat oven to 350°F.

2. Line a cookie sheet with foil.

3. Toss chicken in a large bowl with 1 cup Buffalo Wing Sauce. Season all sides with salt and pepper.

4. Bake 30 to 35 minutes, remove, rest 15 minutes, then shred with two forks or pull apart with your fingers.

5. Toss with remaining Buffalo Wing Sauce.

Whoa, Buffalo: If you just need some shredded chicken, coat the meat with ⅓ cup extra virgin olive oil, then season and bake.

SHREDDED BUFFALO CHICKEN (POACHED/STOVETOP)

PREP TIME: 30 minutes (about 20 active) ★
COOKING TIME: 30 to 35 minutes ★ **YIELD:** 4 to 5 cups

2 cups Buffalo Wing Sauce (page 22)
2 boneless, skinless chicken breasts
5 boneless, skinless chicken thighs
1 to 2 cups chicken stock (if needed)

1. Set a medium-size pot on the stove. Pour 1 cup Buffalo Wing Sauce in pot to completely cover bottom. Arrange one layer of chicken in the pot. Add remaining wing sauce. Add 1 to 2 cups stock, enough to cover.

2. Bring to a boil then adjust heat to a steady simmer. Poach 25 to 30 minutes.

3. Leave poaching liquid in pot and reduce by about a third. Remove chicken and let cool (about 15 minutes).

4. Shred chicken with two forks or pull apart with your fingers.

5. Toss with reduced sauce.

Whoa, Buffalo: For plain poached shredded chicken, pour enough chicken stock in to cover the meat, poach, and discard the liquid. Adjust seasoning.

SHREDDED BUFFALO CHICKEN (SLOW COOKER)

PREP TIME: 15 minutes ★ **COOKING TIME:** 3 to 8 hours ★ **YIELD:** 4 to 5 cups

2 cups Buffalo Wing Sauce (page 22)

2 boneless, skinless chicken breasts

5 boneless, skinless chicken thighs

Kosher salt

Freshly ground black pepper

1. Pour 1 cup Buffalo Wing Sauce in to slow cooker to completely cover bottom. Arrange chicken in one layer as evenly as possible. Top with remaining wing sauce and cover with lid.

2. Set to low and cook 7 to 8 hours or high for 3 to 4 hours. Remove chicken and let cool (about 15 minutes)

3. Shred chicken with two forks or pull apart with your fingers.

4. Toss with ½ cup sauce. Add remaining sauce as necessary and salt and pepper to taste.

Whoa, Buffalo: For plain slow-cooker shredded chicken, add ⅓ cup olive oil and pour enough chicken stock in to cover the meat.

BUFFALO CHICKEN GRILLED CHEESE SANDWICH (PAGE 109)

BUFFALO THIS, BUFFALO THAT, BUFFALO EVERYTHING

◆———◆———◆

Restraint isn't a word typically affiliated with "Buffalo" when you're talking about food. But while there are plenty of comfort food dishes that naturally take to wings' flavor trinity—chicken (fried and otherwise), blue cheese, and Frank's plus butter (pot pie, cream of chicken soup, and French fries, for example)—adding all three components isn't always the best idea. Even when one or two of the flavors really, really work.

Buffalo fried rice sounds delicious, but somehow not so much with blue cheese. Does Buffalo salmon really need any chicken? And while adding a hot sauce component to a wedge salad makes sense, does it really need fried chicken to make a cameo?

You can argue you *always* need fried chicken, but that's an example where sauce and condiment would be better integrated without the main event they're typically associated with.

So, some restraint *can* be required to successfully Buffalo-ize a dish even as you're throwing caution to the wind when seeking out which dishes to riff on. These recipes commandeer and reinterpret some other regional and cultural comfort food icons, integrating Buffalo wings' flavor trinity (or elements of it) into their sauces, soups, and other central elements. If you're looking for inspiration for other great dishes that might be receptive to Buffalo-izing, start here.

BUFFALO WINGS? YES, THEY WAFFLE

There's a waffle iron cookbook called *Will It Waffle?*, that tries to "waffle" just about everything you can imagine. It made me wonder about Buffalo-

izing chicken and waffles and "waffling" a batter with blue cheese. This is one of those recipes that, if you live in one of those houses where you cook

and the person cleans, you may want to help out. Maybe just this once. Waffles are messy, messy stuff. Drips, dots, and crusty bits are par for the course, and the batter bowl always ends up having to get *steaming* hot water and some vigorous scrubbing. And then you add wings, hot sauce, and blue cheese dressing?

Chicken and waffles is one of those classic brunch dishes that I love but I'm really picky about. As delicious as it is, I don't get excited about ordering out at most places. Often, the waffles aren't light enough, and there's something wrong with the chicken—not juicy enough, a bad dredge, not enough seasoning. And it's also just typically a fairly two- to three-note dish, and well, a *brown* one.

If you've got a good handle on making wings, Buffalo-izing this iconic combination is a good solve for that. You get some mild blue in the warm waffle, the guaranteed crispiness of wings, the choice of different sauces for the waffles, and the ease of dismantling those wings.

There will likely be extra batter, which you can store in the fridge for few days for another session, or cook off and freeze in sealable bags to resuscitate in the toaster. You can, of course, just try adding your favorite blue cheese to your go-to prepackage mix, but this make-ahead batter produces light and tasty waffles that should be the last straw in your breakup with Aunt Jemima. (Hey, she never offered to help with the dishes anyway.)

BUFFALO WINGS AND BLUE CHEESE BUTTERMILK WAFFLES

PREP TIME: 3 to 24 hours, and 30 minutes (30 minutes active) ★ **COOKING TIME:** 1 hour ★
YIELD: 12 to 16 waffles and 24 wings

WAFFLES

½ cup warm water (110°F)

1 packet active dry yeast (2¼ teaspoons)

½ cup milk

⅔ cup Saint Agur Blue (or your favorite mild blue cheese)

¾ cup butter

½ teaspoon kosher salt

1 teaspoon sugar

2 cups buttermilk

2½ cups all-purpose flour

2 large eggs, separated

¼ teaspoon baking soda

¼ teaspoon cream of tartar

BUFFALO WINGS

Buffalo Wing Sauce (page 22)

Old-School Buffalo Wings (page 23)

Homemade Blue Cheese Dressing (page 38)

1. Combine warm water and active dry yeast in a very large bowl. Let stand and foam (about 10 to 15 minutes).

2. In a small saucepan over medium heat, combine milk, blue cheese, and ½ cup butter. Warm until butter and cheese melt and milk reaches 120°F, whisking occasionally to combine. Add salt and sugar and dissolve.

3. Lower heat to a simmer. Gradually add in the buttermilk. It will bring the temperature down (maybe even below 110°F).

4. When milk-buttermilk mixture reaches 110°F, remove from heat and add to dissolved yeast. Combine flour, whisking constantly, a little at a time until completely combined (about 3 to 5 minutes).

5. Cover batter with plastic wrap and let rise at least 3 hours (or overnight) at room temperature.

6. When you're ready to make the waffles, remove batter from fridge. Pre-heat fryer to 350 to 355°F for the wings, and the oven at 250°F to keep the waffles warm (unless you plan to serve them as you make 'em).

7. Separate eggs and reserve whites. Add baking soda to yolks, beat, then gently fold into batter.

8. Prepare Buffalo Wing Sauce, Old-School Buffalo Wings, and Blue Cheese Dressing.

9. Heat the waffle iron and melt remaining ¼ cup butter.

10. Add cream of tartar to whites, and, using a hand mixer, stand mixer, or good

continued

old-fashioned human arm mixer, whisk egg whites to stiff peaks. Gently fold egg whites into batter to thoroughly combine. Try to maintain as much height as possible to the batter.

11. Using a brush or paper towel dipped in butter, coat the iron's griddles. Ladle ½ to ¾ cup batter per waffle into the iron. Remember, it'll spread! So, for the first one, start with just ½ cup until you know how much you'll really need. Cook according to manufacturer's instructions, until both sides are just more than slightly golden brown and no longer stick to the iron (about 3 to 6 minutes).

12. Repeat until all the waffles and wings are made (storing them in the preheated oven), or until you can't hold off the mob at the gates.

13. Serve waffle topped with six wings, a drizzle of Blue Cheese Dressing and Buffalo Wing Sauce, or sides of both.

Sweet and Savory: Some people like their savory with a little sweet, especially when it comes to fried chicken and waffles. Consider holding the blue cheese dressing and serving the waffles with butter and some maple syrup mixed with Frank's RedHot sauce (figure on about one part Frank's to three parts syrup).

Mom Always Said to Share: As *Buffalo News* food editor Andrew Galarneau pointed out to me, this dish is really a no-brainer for sharing. Cut the waffle into its four sections and pile each with two to three wings for a great share plate.

MORE AMERICAN THAN APPLE PIE

Whether in the toaster oven or in a pan on the stove, grilled cheese is one of the first things many of us as Americans learn how to cook. The alchemy that happens when butter and heat interact with bread is an amazing thing. Starting at about nine years old, I'd slather more butter than could possibly be healthy on all sides of sliced bread, and then put them in the toaster on low, moderating the temperature, watching intently with my chin on the counter in front of it as the heating coils turned red, the butter melted into the bread and turned gold, then brown.

Cheese adds yet another dimension, and there's nothing about that magic that doesn't translate to any age. As I discovered all those years ago, the key to a great grilled cheese is patience: cook it low and slow, albeit in a pan. This can make it a 25-minute process, but the result is cheese oozing out the side, crusty delayed gratification.

Grilled cheese recipes and preferred ingredients can be deeply personal, passionately held beliefs. White American or Cheddar? Single cheese, or a blend? Slices or shredded? If slices, how many? And what kind of bread? See? You had answers, or at least, images of preferences of each of these flash through your head. And these factors can affect cooking time. So just remember, low, slow, and patience. For the record: white

American *and* Cheddar, slices if it's a straight-up grilled cheese (at least four), and either Pullman loaf, sourdough, or Martin's potato bread (or rolls). And if you're going with the rolls, do the reverse-griddle where you cook the outer part of the bun first and end with it facing the cheese at the center.

The secret to *this* recipe is use pimento cheese draped with the sliced stuff, but to add shredded chicken—Buffalo Chicken Pimento Cheese Salad (page 151)—a great sandwich in and of itself. That mix of shredded and sliced ensures terrific cheese and chicken integration post-melt and a guaranteed cheese pull.

═ BUFFALO CHICKEN GRILLED CHEESE SANDWICH ═

PREP TIME: 15 to 25 minutes (depending on if you serve with dipping sauces) ★
COOKING TIME: 25 minutes ★ **YIELD:** 2 sandwiches

4 to 6 teaspoons mayonnaise (for homemade, page 100)

4 slices of your favorite bread for grilled cheese sandwiches

3 tablespoons butter

4 slices white American cheese

4 slices mozzarella

1 cup Buffalo Chicken Pimento Cheese Salad (page 151)

¼ cup Buffalo Wing Sauce (page 22, optional)

⅔ cup Homemade Blue Cheese Dressing for dipping (page 38, optional)

1. Spread mayo evenly on both sides of every slice of bread (½ to 1 teaspoon mayo per side).

2. Heat a large cast-iron pan or seasoned skillet big enough to hold four slices over medium-low heat. When hot, coat entire surface with 1½ tablespoons butter. Place four bread slices in the center of the pan and toast gently until the bottoms are crisp and colored, then flip (about 3 minutes per side).

3. Layer one slice of white American and mozzarella on each slice of bread. Evenly distribute a quarter of the Buffalo chicken pimento cheese salad on each slice of bread in the pan covering all surfaces, then lower heat, cover, and cook until mixture has turned melty, about 15 minutes. (This is when to add more cheese slices if you dare.)

4. Combine halves, cover, turn heat up slightly, and griddle until bottom is golden brown (1 to 2 minutes), then flip, repeat, and remove.

5. Let sandwiches cool 1 to 2 minutes, then slice, and, if using, serve with Blue Cheese Dressing and Buffalo Wing Sauce for dipping.

Wow Factor: Instead of serving with blue cheese dressing and wing sauce, try this with a bowl of Cream of Buffalo Wing Soup (page 124).

WHY DID THE CHICKEN CROSS THE ROAD? TO GET IN THE CHICKEN POT PIE

Like grilled cheese, chicken pot pie can be a pretty personal thing. Whether it's mom's or your guilty pleasure grocery brand, it's a dish many Americans have childhood associations with. That means there are myriad ways to make it. I believe there are *five* keys to the ultimate chicken pot pie. There needs to be *enough* pastry; the sauce needs to be velvety (not runny); the chicken shouldn't be overcooked before being added to the filling; it should be cut in three different sizes for proper distribution and bite satisfaction; and the veg should be added raw, or practically raw, before the

pie is cooked so its textural variation is actually a *presence*.

You can nerd out even more over the crust! Should you make your own? Should there be a crust bottom? Individual portions or one big pie? It's not *hard* to make your own pie crust, but I'm a fan of an airy and buttery *puff pastry*. That involves lots of folding and temperature controlling butter, which I usually don't have time for. So I turn to Dufour Pastry Kitchens. Theirs is great. (They also make a chocolate one . . . what!?)

Some places just ladle filling in a bowl and cover

it with a biscuit top or a floating pastry cover. Why would you do that to people? It's a pie! It should have a top and bottom! I like *lots* of crust, and a ratio of crust-to-filling that leaves me somewhere between stuffed and unable to resist another helping anyway, so as you can tell, I'm a top-and-bottom pastry man and a proponent of individual portions. But when I make pot pie, I *usually* make enough for my wife and me to eat all week, or for a party, and use a big baking dish.

This recipe requires a little work, but most of it's chopping, and trust me, it's worth it!

BUFFALO CHICKEN POT PIE

PREP TIME: 45 minutes ★ **COOKING TIME:** 1 hour and 30 minutes ★ **SERVES:** 6 people

2 packages Dufour pastry

4 chicken breasts

5 teaspoons extra virgin olive oil

5 tablespoons Frank's RedHot Sauce

Kosher salt

Freshly ground black pepper

¾ cup unsalted butter

5 cloves garlic, minced

2 large onions, chopped

2 poblano peppers, chopped

1 red bell pepper, chopped

1 jalapeño, minced

4 celery stalks, chopped

2 large carrots, chopped

¾ cup flour

4 cups chicken stock

1 cup heavy cream

1 tablespoons minced fresh thyme

2 tablespoons minced fresh dill

½ pound Saint Agur Blue

1 cup frozen peas

1. Defrost the pastry in the fridge 2 to 3 hours. Preheat oven to 500°F.

2. Meanwhile, place chicken in a foil-lined baking pan. Toss chicken breasts with oil, 2 tablespoons of hot sauce, salt, and pepper. Roast 10 minutes, then remove, let cool, and cube large, medium, and small. Reserve juices.

3. Warm a large saucepan over medium heat and melt the butter. Add all the garlic, half the onions, poblano, red bell pepper, jalapeño, celery, and carrots, and simmer 5 minutes over medium heat until onions start to become translucent.

4. Add flour and cook over low heat for 3 minutes, stirring. Add reserved juices from cooking the chicken as well as the stock, then simmer, stirring until flour disappears and mixture thickens.

continued

5. Add heavy cream, 3 tablespoons hot sauce, and herbs, and salt and pepper to taste.

6. Adjust oven temperature to 375°F. Rub butter along insides of a deep baking tray (about 1 foot long and 3 inches tall) or individual oven-safe bowls. Then line the bottom with pastry.

7. Divide the blue cheese into four quarters. Scatter one half as evenly as possible over the pastry. Parcook until puffy (about 15 minutes) and remove.

8. Toss reserved vegetables (including the remaining onions and peas), and half the cubed chicken into the filling mixture. Mix well.

9. Layer filling onto the pastry halfway up the baking dish. Scatter another quarter of the blue cheese evenly across filling. Evenly scatter remaining chicken, then top with remaining filling.

10. Cover with pastry, brush the top with egg wash, scatter remaining quarter of blue cheese on top, and season with salt and pepper. Pierce with a knife or fork prongs in a few places.

11. Bake 45 minutes to 1 hour, until pastry top is golden brown and cooked through.

12. Remove and let settle for 15 minutes, then serve.

BUFFALO DISCO FRIES

Know someone who loves the nightlife who is from New Jersey? Want to start a fight? Go ahead and tell them you invented disco fries. The dish, if you're unfamiliar with it, has been one of the state's most famous post-clubbing hangover panaceas and preventatives for at least a few decades, and it's easy to see why. French fries, melted cheese, and brown gravy, hot and crisped under a broiler, soft and saucy in places, crusty and crunchy in others—that has comfort food written all over it. (Unlike poutine, disco fries do *not* include cheese curds—they're not the same thing.) The name of the dish, the story goes, came about in the mid-'70s to early '80s because it was the signature late-night meal of the disco crowd. And the Tick Tock Diner in Clifton, NJ (founded in 1948), is their gravy-soaked Mecca.

Various people over the years have claimed they invented the dish, noting that while cheese fries and a cup of gravy were both on the menu, *they* were the first to combine them. *Saveur* cites Chef Pat Romano as saying he first heard the term in the early 1990s while partying at bars in Manhattan and North Jersey. Fair enough. But among my social circle, my friend Jenn Ayres makes a different claim. "I didn't invent disco fries," she's said repeatedly and without any self-doubt. "I just coined the term."

Jenn, who is known for using her oven to store her sweaters, says that in the '80s, she used to go to all the "diners and late-night food places Downtown for 'French Fries Deluxe' after going to clubs." She says they would *always* come with cheese, but sometimes also topped with or accompanied by a side of gravy.

When they *didn't* come with gravy she'd ask for a side, and when it *was* topped with it, she'd ask for it on the side because some didn't make great gravy.

"I just started calling them disco fries over and over, all over Downtown," Jenn has told us. "We were just dancing all night. Then it just came out: 'Gotta go get my disco fries.' I started in the '80s and did it until I left for LA in 1994. It stuck. Those same places started calling them disco fries on their menus. One time, I came back from LA to go clubbing and we went to one of the old diners in the East Village at 5:30 AM and it was on the menu. It wasn't called 'French Fries Deluxe' anymore. This is my contribution to society."

Needless to say, there are a few skeptics. I don't have a horse in that game. Neither do I claim to be the first to Buffalo-ize fries, but the recipe below is my riff on the tastiest way to Buffalo-ize disco fries. Most people will say that to be authentic they need to be steak fries and the cheese needs to be mozzarella. I use mozzarella, but mix it into a sauce with provolone and blue cheese to add a little more flavor. I also substitute wing sauce for gravy and add a few other classic wing elements (celery and blue cheese dressing) along with Buffalo-ized bacon, because . . . why not.

But when I needed someone to name them, I knew there was only one person to turn to. "'Speed Metal Fries,'" Jenn said matter-of-factly. Why? "Because it sounds cooler than disco fries."

Thanks, Jenn. And now there's no doubt about where this name came from.

SPEED METAL FRIES

PREP TIME: 45 minutes ★ **COOKING TIME:** 1 hour ★ **SERVES:** 4 people

2 cups Buffalo Wing Sauce (page 22)

2½ cups Homemade Blue Cheese Dressing (page 23)

½ cup crumbled Buffalo-ized Bacon (page 97, optional)

2 chicken thighs, skin on

Kosher salt

Freshly ground black pepper

6 cups crinkle cut French fries

1 tablespoon butter

1 tablespoon flour

⅔ cup milk

3 ounces crumbled Saint Agur Blue

3 ounces shredded provolone

5 ounces shredded mozzarella

2 celery stalks, peeled and shaved (or minced)

2 large carrots, peeled and shaved (or minced)

1. Preheat oven to 425°F or fryer to 350°F and line a cookie sheet with paper towels.

2. Meanwhile, prepare Buffalo Wing Sauce, Blue Cheese Dressing, and optional crumbled Buffalo-ized Bacon.

3. Turn the chicken thigh skin side down on the cutting board. Find the bone. Make incisions along both sides of the bone. Slide the knife beneath the bone and slice the meat from the bone and remove it. Repeat with second thigh, then season with salt and pepper.

4. Fry chicken 7 to 8 minutes then remove and reserve.

continued

5. If you're frying the fries, lower oil temperature to 300°F. If you're going to fry, cook for 3 minutes at 300°F. Remove fries, drain, and rest on paper towel–lined tray. Raise oil temperature to 375°F. When oil reaches 375°F, drop fries back in again 4 to 5 minutes or until crispy, golden, and brown. Remove, drain, and toss them in a large bowl with a pinch of salt. Remove to the paper towel–lined cookie sheet. If you're baking the fries, line another cookie sheet with foil and lightly coat it with cooking spray, or place a baking rack above it. Spread fries out on the sheet (or the rack) so none touch. Bake 30 minutes, then toss them in a large bowl with a pinch of salt and remove to the paper towel–lined cookie sheet.

6. While fries are cooking, make a roux: In a medium saucepan over medium heat, melt butter. Add flour and whisk to combine until sandy (3 minutes). Add milk and whisk constantly until thoroughly combined and mixture bubbles and thickens (4 minutes).

7. Gradually add 2 ounces each of blue, provolone, and mozzarella cheeses to mixture and mix until thoroughly combined (3 minutes). Season with salt and pepper.

8. Turn broiler to medium.

9. Set out four oven-safe bowls and coat bottoms with wing sauce. Fill each halfway with fries then pour cheese sauce over to create an evenly coated layer. Drizzle wing sauce over cheese sauce in each. Finish filling each bowl with fries.

10. Cut fried chicken thighs into pieces about the size of a dime. Scatter chicken on top of the fries. Pour wing sauce over to create an evenly coated layer in each. Pour over remaining cheese sauce in each bowl.

11. Evenly scatter remaining shredded provolone and mozzarella cheese on top. Then place bowls under the broiler for 3 minutes.

12. Remove (careful!) bowls, drizzle wing sauce over the top (*now* forget caution), garnish with celery, carrots, and crumbled blue, and drizzle with blue cheese dressing.

13. Serve with any remaining wing sauce and blue cheese dressing on the side.

THE *REASON* TO HAVE LEFTOVER RICE

I rarely order fried rice when out at restaurants or when we do delivery Chinese. In my house, I always make it the day *after* we order Chinese food. We rarely eat much of the white rice the night we order food (it just feels like filler), and have gotten into the habit of turning it into a "free" meal the next night for dinner (with leftovers for lunch the following day too!). That falls in line with the purported birth of the dish: that it originated out of the need to use day-old rice so as not to waste food.

And fried rice, a dish that, in turn, can also transform other leftovers into a main event, is the perfect vehicle for wing sauce, chicken, celery, and wings' occasional other accompaniment, carrots. While you do want to use sesame and vegetable oil to stir-fry the chicken, vegetables, and rice, butter-based wing sauce adheres marvelously to everything when tossed with it all at the end. If this sounds weird, I get it, but it's a sponge for flavor and a natural fit for the flavor profile and any wingnut's wing ingredient leftovers.

While this recipe certainly falls in the category of dishes you can make with leftover rice, things you pretty much always have in the fridge (butter and hot sauce), and a few other freezer staples, I have to be honest: it's too good to wait until the next chance occasion you happen to have leftover rice. You're going to want to either order some Chinese food to make it (maybe insane, but what I do), or make some rice. Just in case it's the latter, those steps are included in the recipe below too.

BUFFALO FRIED RICE

PREP TIME: 30 minutes ★ **COOKING TIME:** 40 minutes ★ **YIELD:** 4 cups

1 tablespoon sesame oil

2 tablespoons soy sauce

4 tablespoons sesame seeds

1¼ teaspoons kosher salt, divided

2 cups white rice (preferably leftover from the night before)

8 tablespoons vegetable oil

4 boneless, skinless chicken thighs, cubed small

1 white onion, minced

3 large carrots, peeled and diced

3 celery stalks, peeled and diced

6 cloves garlic, minced

2 eggs, whisked

1 cup peas

5 tablespoons finely chopped parsley

⅔ cup Buffalo Wing Sauce (page 22)

1 bunch scallions, chopped

1 cup crumbled Buffalo-ized Bacon bits (page 97)

1. In a pot with a tight-fitting lid, bring 1¾ cups water to a boil.

2. Mix sesame oil and soy sauce and reserve.

3. Warm a wok or a large skillet over high heat. Add sesame seeds. Cook 30 seconds then remove and reserve.

4. If you don't have leftover rice, add 1 teaspoon salt and rice to boiling water, stir once, then cover with a tight lid. Turn heat to low and simmer 18 minutes, then turn off and let rice steam for 5 minutes.

5. Add 2 tablespoons vegetable oil to pan and let it get smoking hot. Add cubed chicken and cook 4 minutes, stirring halfway through. Remove and reserve.

6. Add 2 tablespoons vegetable oil to pan and get it smoking hot. Add half the rice, and cook, stirring occasionally, for 3 minutes. Remove and reserve fried rice. Repeat with remaining rice. Remove and reserve.

7. Add 2 tablespoons vegetable oil to pan and get it smoking hot. Add onion, carrots, celery, and garlic, then cook 3 minutes. Remove and reserve.

8. Get pan smoking hot. Reintroduce rice, chicken, and vegetables and push up against the sides of the pan, clearing a well in the center. Add 2 tablespoons vegetable oil to center. After 1 minute, add eggs. Scramble eggs with a wooden spoon or spatula.

9. Add peas, ¼ teaspoon salt, 4 tablespoons parsley, sesame oil–soy mixture, and Buffalo Wing Sauce, then toss rice to thoroughly coat everything. Cook 2 minutes. Serve immediately and garnish with sesame seeds, chopped scallions, remaining parsley, and crumbled bacon.

COMFORT FOOD COLLISION

Like chicken pot pie, mac & cheese is one of those dishes we all have strong opinions about. While one can argue about the pluses and minuses of bread crumbs, the merits and time-consuming nature of making a béchamel, and who makes the best boxed mac & cheese, two things are without debate: It's quite possibly the ultimate American comfort food, and if you're making some, you better make lots.

This recipe riffs on a very popular online version by Martha Stewart, which many folks have dubbed the best on the Internet. There's not much that's difficult about this recipe, but it does involve making a white sauce to bind all the ingredients together. If you want to cut the cooking time, buy a rotisserie chicken.

BUFFALO CHICKEN MAC & CHEESE

PREP TIME: 35 minutes ★ **COOKING TIME:** 1 hour and 20 minutes ★ **SERVES:** 12 people

¾ cup butter, plus more for casserole dish

2 cups Shredded Buffalo Chicken (page 101)

1 small onion, minced

2 carrots, grated

2 stalks celery, finely sliced

3 cloves garlic, minced

2 jalapeños, minced

5 slices white bread, crusts removed, rough chopped in tiny squares

Kosher salt

4 cups penne

½ cup flour

5 cups whole milk

¼ teaspoon cayenne

¼ teaspoon mustard powder

4½ cups grated sharp white Cheddar

2 cups grated Gruyère

6 tablespoons crumbled Saint Agur Blue

¼ teaspoon freshly ground black pepper

4 tablespoons Frank's RedHot Sauce (or to taste)

1. Preheat oven to 400°F and cover large pot of water and bring to a boil.

2. Butter a deep casserole dish and set aside.

3. Prepare Shredded Buffalo Chicken.

4. For the carrot and celery garnish: Melt 3 tablespoons butter over medium heat. Add onion and sauté until translucent. Add carrots, celery, garlic, and jalapeño, mix well, and sauté 3 minutes. Combine with Shredded Buffalo Chicken and reserve.

5. For bread crumbs: In a saucepan, melt 4 tablespoons of butter. Toss cut bread in butter and reserve.

6. For the pasta: Salt boiling water until it tastes like the sea. Cook pasta until al dente, drain in a colander, and rinse with cold running water. Drain and reserve.

continued

7. For the cheese sauce: Melt 6 tablespoons butter in a large saucepan over medium heat. Add flour and whisk until sandy and starts to turn golden. Add milk to roux, whisking continuously until smooth and it comes to a boil. Then lower heat, cooking for a total of 10 minutes. Add cayenne, mustard powder, 3½ cups Cheddar, 1½ cup Gruyère, and Saint Agur. Stir 2 minutes until thoroughly combined, then remove from heat.

8. To assemble: In a large bowl, add Buffalo chicken mixture, pasta, and cheese sauce. Mix gently until well combined. Adjust seasoning with salt, pepper, and Frank's (!).

9. Fill casserole dish. Sprinkle remaining cheese on top, then scatter bread crumbs evenly over surface.

10. Bake 35 minutes, until golden brown. Remove from oven, rest 5 minutes, then serve.

EASY, UNFORGETTABLE BUFFALO SALMON

My friend Stacey Glick's husband Jeremy is from Buffalo. She told me that at *their* house, far more things than *wings* get Buffalo-ized for dinner. An *Epicurious* recipe for Buffalo salmon long ago found its way onto their table and has made many, many repeat appearances ever since. No wonder! It's zippy, delicious, and, at under 30 minutes to make, is an easy centerpiece to a meal that pairs easily with whatever vegetables or sides you like. (Though it's hard to believe anyone will be paying much attention to anything but the fish.)

If you feel like geeking out with Buffalo sauce (and don't mind complicating the recipe slightly), consider making Buffalo Bread Crumbs (page 98) to top the salmon with. If the bread crumbs are meant to mimic crispy wing skin, it only makes sense, right?

BUFFALO SALMON

PREP TIME: 8 minutes ★ **COOKING TIME:** 15 to 25 minutes ★ **YIELD:** 2 salmon filets

1 cup Buffalo Wing Sauce (page 22)
3 tablespoons vegetable oil
⅔ cup Buffalo Panko (page 98)
Two 1-pound salmon filets (with skin on)
Kosher salt
Freshly ground black pepper

1. Preheat oven to 425°F. (Make sure to place a rack high up in the oven.)

2. Prepare Buffalo Wing Sauce. Reserve a third of sauce to serve with fish.

3. Use 1 tablespoon oil to lightly grease a shallow baking pan.

4. Toss Buffalo Panko with 2 tablespoons oil.

5. Put salmon filets, skin side down, in baking pan an inch or two apart. Brush top and sides of each filet with two thirds of the Buffalo Wing Sauce. Sprinkle filets with salt and pepper, then evenly cover the top of each with Buffalo Panko.

6. Bake 15 to 22 minutes, until panko has turned golden brown and the fish is *just* cooked. Serve with remaining third of Buffalo Wing Sauce.

BUFFALO . . . SALAD?
WEDGING BELLS ARE RINGING

It's not as though there's *no* way to integrate chicken into a Buffalo wedge salad. I've seen it done. And far be it from me to say you shouldn't make one for yourself with a side of Shredded Buffalo Chicken (page 101), or a fanned out, sliced, sautéed breast, or roasted chicken cubes tossed in or drizzled with sauce, or with a pounded-thin fried chicken cutlet painted with wing sauce leaning up against the side of the wedge.

But part of the appeal of this salad has always been that it's a honking quarter-chunk of lettuce on a plate. Dripping with dressing, sure, with little nuggets of blue cheese perched on the edge of ice-berg cliffs about to tumble off into a pool of minced green onions and bacon, and, depending on the chef, a few other flourishes here and there—but otherwise fairly unadulterated. After all, your steak's on the way, right?

So, this recipe doesn't call for chicken. It integrates wing sauce into the quick-pickled onions and bacon so you get zesty bites that rescue you momentarily from the blue cheese dressing undertow. Just don't forget a few drops of hot sauce over the finished salad as garnish and a little extra punctuation.

BUFFALO WEDGE SALAD

PREP TIME: 50 minutes ★ **COOKING TIME:** 20 minutes ★ **Serves:** 4 people

¼ white onion, sliced thin

¼ tablespoon Frank's RedHot Sauce

9 slices Buffalo-ized Bacon, crumbled (page 97)

1½ to 2 cups Homemade Blue Cheese Dressing (page 38)

1 head iceberg lettuce, quartered

20 cherry tomatoes, halved

20 dill fronds, for garnish

Minced chives, for garnish

4 spring onions, chopped, for garnish

½ celery stalk, quartered and minced

1 large carrot, peeled, quartered, and minced

½ teaspoon celery seeds

Freshly ground black pepper

1. Slice onions as thinly as you can. Submerge in Frank's RedHot Sauce.

2. Prepare Buffalo-ized Bacon and Blue Cheese Dressing.

3. Drizzle Blue Cheese Dressing over the top and sides of lettuce wedge, trying to get some inside lettuce crevices. Top and surround with cherry tomato halves.

4. Garnish with five to six onion slices per salad. Reserve the hot sauce the onions had been pickling in.

5. Garnish with bacon, dill, chives, spring onions, celery, carrot, and celery seeds.

6. Drizzle four to five drops of reserved hot sauce, season with fresh pepper, and serve.

BUFFALO, BY WAY OF PITTSBURGH

Pittsburgh's just a three-hour drive south of Buffalo. And it's sent the "almost famous" coleslaw- and French fry–laden sandwiches from Primanti Bros., its most iconic restaurant, to Buffalo (the Bills beat the Jets, giving the Steelers a shot at the playoffs). So, cross-pollination of the cities' food icons shouldn't be a huge surprise. Indeed, there are wings on Primanti's menu (though their breading should be anathema to any Nickel City resident). And there's even a Buffalo chicken sandwich, albeit under its "other sandwiches" section where they don't come with both slaw and fries. But the inspiration is there to Buffalo-ize the Burgh.

But which sandwich? Primanti features at least 20 meat combinations including pastrami, corned beef, roast beef, bologna, and sardines. The most well-known is probably the "Pitts-burger & cheese" (the "#2 best seller"), a seasoned hamburger steak. You could very well do a ground chicken or turkey version, or a grilled chicken or turkey breast, all doused with wing sauce. But let's face it—it's hard to get excited about a turkey burger or a grilled chicken sandwich. A piece of fried chicken doused in wing sauce though? Maybe topped with a few slices of butter-griddled capicola, one of the signature moves at Primanti? Now that's something you could get behind.

PRIMANTI SANDWICH, BUFFALO-STYLE

PREP TIME: 2 hours (1 hour active) ★ **COOKING TIME:** 35 to 55 minutes ★ **YIELD:** 2 sandwiches

8 cups Buffalo Coleslaw (page 157)

1 cup Buffalo Wing Sauce (page 22)

2½ cups Homemade Blue Cheese Dressing (page 38)

2 large Russet potatoes, skin on, and well-cleaned

2 cups buttermilk (or 2 cups pickle brine)

2¾ tablespoons kosher salt

2¼ teaspoons freshly ground black pepper

2 boneless, skinless chicken thighs

1 cup flour

1 teaspoon cayenne

4 cups peanut oil

2 tablespoons butter

4 slices capicola

2 teaspoons mayonnaise (for homemade, page 100)

4 slices soft, 1-inch thick Italian loaf

4 slices provolone

4 slices tomato

6 slices onion

1. Make a batch of Buffalo Coleslaw.

2. Prepare batches of Buffalo Wing Sauce and Blue Cheese Dressing.

3. Cut potatoes into fries ¼ inch thick. Soak in cold water in the fridge for 1 hour.

4. Meanwhile, mix buttermilk with 2 tablespoons salt and 1 teaspoon black pepper. Soak chicken in mixture for 1 hour.

5. Mix flour, ½ tablespoon salt, 1 teaspoon black pepper, and cayenne in a brown paper bag (or a bowl).

6. Bring peanut oil to 325°F in a cast-iron skillet with a lid (or set your fryer).

7. Line a baking sheet with paper towels near the oil. Drain and dry fries with paper towels, then gently drop potatoes into the oil and fry 5 minutes (until they turn a light blond). Remove fries with a strainer to the paper towel–lined sheet.

8. Raise the oil temperature to 350°F.

9. Place wet chicken thighs in the paper bag, crumple the top closed and shake to cover. Remove and gently shake off any excess dredge.

10. Line a baking sheet with paper towels and place near the oil. If using cast iron, fry chicken 15 minutes (covered), flip, then cook 5 to 15 more minutes. If using your fryer, cook to manufacturer's instructions (about 15 to 20 minutes). Remove the paper towel–lined sheet.

11. Raise oil temperature to 375°F. Drop fries into oil and fry another 3 to 5 minutes. Remove to paper towels and season with salt.

12. Melt butter in a large saucepan over medium heat. Place one capicola slice in each quarter of the pan so they're not touching. Cook 2 minutes, flip, and cook 2 more minutes.

13. Spread mayonnaise on two slices of bread. Coat chicken thighs with Buffalo Wing Sauce.

14. Next, layer the sandwich. Start with the fried chicken on top of the slice spread with mayo. Top with two slices of capicola, two slices of cheese, half the fries, ½ cup slaw, two tomato slices, four slices onion, and three tablespoons Blue Cheese Dressing. Top with a mayo-less bread slice.

15. Repeat, wrap sandwiches in wax paper, cut sandwiches in half, and serve.

By Request: Onions are by request at Primanti but they're always a nice touch. So is a fried egg, which adds a little more "sauce" to the mix to make it messier, wetter, and thus, a little bit easier to eat the whole thing. If you do add egg, the correct way to layer it is on top of the cheese.

THE SOUP THAT EATS LIKE A BOWL OF WINGS

Along with tomato and cream of mushroom, cream of chicken has to be one of the most popular canned soups. It delivers all the nurse-yourself-comfort of classic chicken soup bite after silky-smooth bite. And what's that you say? It's pretty much stock, bits of shredded chicken, celery, and . . . butter? The perfect canvas. How has this not been Buffalo-ized?

Oh right, of course it has: "Kickin' Buffalo-Style Chicken," by the savvy folks at Campbell's ("the soup that eats like a meal" kind) no less, adding potato, celery, carrots, cayenne pepper sauce, red peppers,

and Cheddar. Gotta be honest, there's a time and place for canned condensed soups, but in my house that place is relegated to the past (my childhood in the '80s) and as ingredients in the occasional casserole. Otherwise, we're a homemade soup kind of house, even if sometimes, when the bills means made-on-a-budget, that's a riff on stone soup.

This one's zippy, creamy, and perfect for a cold winter day, maybe with a Buffalo Chicken Grilled Cheese Sandwich (page 109) to dip into it. And it's so easy to make—pretty much just roast (chicken), cut (vegetables), and simmer (everything).

═════════ CREAM OF BUFFALO WING SOUP ═════════

PREP TIME: 20 minutes ★ **COOKING TIME:** 1 hour and 20 minutes ★ **YIELD:** 14 cups

1 pound chicken breasts

1 pound chicken thighs (skinless and boneless)

½ cup Buffalo Wing Sauce (page 22)

Kosher salt

Freshly ground black pepper

2 tablespoons butter

2 medium onions, diced

4 to 6 celery stalks, diced

3 medium carrots, diced

4 cloves garlic, minced

3 tablespoons all-purpose flour

8 cups chicken broth

1 cup heavy cream

½ cup sour cream

¼ cup Homemade Blue Cheese Dressing (page 38)

½ cup Frank's RedHot Sauce

¾ cup crumbled blue cheese

3 scallions, diced

9 slices Buffalo-ized Bacon (page 97, optional)

1. Preheat oven to 400°F.

2. Set a baking tray over a foil-lined sheet tray. Brush breast and thigh meat on all sides with Buffalo Wing Sauce. Season all sides with salt and pepper. Place on baking tray and put tray in the oven for 35 minutes.

3. In a large pot, melt butter over medium heat. Add onions, 1 cup each celery, carrots, and garlic. Cook 3 to 5 minutes until vegetables start to soften.

4. Sprinkle flour over vegetables, stir well, and cook until flour turns slightly golden (about 3 minutes).

5. Stir in chicken broth and dissolve flour mixture.

6. In a large bowl, add heavy cream, sour cream, Blue Cheese Dressing, and Frank's RedHot. Whisk vigorously until completely combined. Add mixture to pot and stir 5 minutes to thoroughly combine.

7. Add ½ cup blue cheese, stir soup, then simmer it on medium 30 minutes.

8. Serve soup and garnish with reserved carrots, celery, crumbled blue cheese, and optional Buffalo-ized Bacon.

BUFFALO ROCK SHRIMP (PAGE 133)

RINGS, STICKERS & OTHER APPS

◆━━━━━◆━━━━━◆

I'm sure there are appetizers that won't "Buffalo." I just keep thinking of the ones that do—deviled eggs, popcorn shrimp, potstickers, twice-baked potatoes—anything already delicious and addictive that you've been served on a passed plate can be made better with a little streak of Buffalo. And while I'm already going to a special place in hell reserved for carnivores who talk out of the other side of their mouths about seitan, I must say that Buffalo wings' signature flavor is just as successful in transforming tempeh, tofu, broccoli, and cauliflower as it is with meat. If you like these recipes, trying to figure out how to make even more things Buffalo—like Buffalo meatballs, pigs in a blanket, and jalapeño poppers—has to be in your future.

TASTES LIKE CHICKEN

I was a skeptic and I wasn't going to do it. But our friend Deb Perelman was procrastinating from working on her recipe site *Smitten Kitchen* one day and suggested including a recipe for Buffalo broccoli and cauliflower. I was curious about how good it could possibly be. We had some Texan family friends over one night, Danny Sanchez and Lisa DeLeon (a vegetarian), who took one for the team as taste-testers. After a few suggestions from Lisa and several trials, Danny was convinced you wouldn't be able to tell the difference if I snuck one of these in a basket of boneless wings in a dark bar. That's when my wife Angela said, "Tastes like chicken."

I don't know about all that (there *was* wine involved) but I gotta tell you: *this* is how I now eat cauliflower. Know though that if you're not a vegetarian, making these means you love the folks you're making them for. To do them right, you really need the patience and time to thoroughly coat each floret. That love shows up with all the little cracks and crevices on each "wing."

A few other pointers:

★ You need a four-step dredge station (buttermilk, Wondra, egg, then corn flake dust) to create the coating that makes the florets resemble wings.

- ★ Unless you want to make so much of each dredge that everything will be completely submerged, you'll want a clean spoon to help coat the florets at each stage.
- ★ Fried is better than baked (shocking, I know).
- ★ You could do all cauliflower or all broccoli, but just like a plate of wings comes with drums and flats, the variation is nice.
- ★ Serve immediately after tossing in sauce. Like real wings, the longer they sit, the more they lose crunch.

I know, I know, crunchy "vegetable chicken skin"? Sounds dubious. But these *are* a winner.

BROCCOLI AND CAULIFLOWER "WINGS"

PREP TIME: 40 minutes ★ **COOKING TIME:** 20 to 35 minutes ★ **YIELD:** 24 "wings"

1 cup Buffalo Wing Sauce (page 22)

3 cups corn flakes

3 eggs

1½ cups Wondra flour

1 teaspoon kosher salt

1 teaspoon white pepper

1 cup buttermilk

12 broccoli florets, cut to resemble drumsticks

12 cauliflower florets, cut to resemble drumsticks

1 cup Homemade Blue Cheese Dressing (page 38)

4 stalks celery, peeled and cut 2 inches long

1. Make Buffalo Wing Sauce.

2. Pulse corn flakes in a blender until they completely turn to dust. Beat the eggs until completely yellow. Then combine Wondra flour with salt and pepper.

3. Set up a dredge station with four bowls or containers: first buttermilk, then flour, then beaten eggs, and finally the corn flake dust.

4. If you're baking, preheat oven to 450°F. If you're frying, preheat fryer to 355°F (or fill a high-edged pot or skillet with enough vegetable or canola oil to cover a batch of six florets).

5. Using a fork or spoon, toss three florets at a time in buttermilk, tilting the container to submerge in one corner if necessary to soak all the inner crevices. Without piercing or breaking, remove from buttermilk to Wondra. Gently toss and turn to coat completely with flour (using a clean spoon to cover the florets with flour works really well). Remove florets to the beaten egg and cover on all sides, using another clean spoon again to get at all the crevices. Remove to corn flake dust, using a spoon to completely coat. Reserve on a cooling rack above a foil-lined cookie tray. Repeat until done.

6. If you're baking, put the "wings" in oven for 35 minutes, checking for doneness in the last 5 minutes. If you're frying, fry batches of six (three broccoli

and three cauliflower) at 355°F for 3 to 5 minutes, depending on how crispy you like them.

7. Toss in Buffalo Wing Sauce and serve with Blue Cheese Dressing and celery immediately.

THE KILLER B'S: BUFFALO BOMBS AWAY

Man, I love homemade biscuits. Fresh from the oven? Forget chocolate chip cookies—if I ever walk into an open house where they've been baking biscuits . . . that'd be it. Sold. You get those flaky, buttery layers, the steam that sneaks out as you dig your thumb in and lift one half off. The drips of butter that roll off when a cold pat gets spread over that fresh, steaming surface . . . excuse me while I go make a batch.

For years, whenever I've made biscuits, that's meant the recipe by Edna Lewis and Scott Peacock in *The Gift of Southern Cooking*. But I have to admit, I'm pretty non-discriminatory when it comes to homemade biscuits—I'd be lying if I said I wouldn't devour Bisquick biscuits fresh from the oven too. That's all to say that I won't tell anyone, or look down on you if you use a prepackaged mix or the store-bought rolls sold in cans by the dairy section. But if you're into trying legit southern-style biscuits, you'll want to try this recipe on its own at least once.

Of course, using Edna's recipe to make biscuits stuffed with Buffalo chicken and wrapped with bacon may seem like sacrilege to some. Sure, maybe it's also completely un-southern. But they taste really good. Just make sure not to overfill them, and to serve them piping hot.

═══ BUFFALO CHICKEN BACON BISCUIT BOMBS ═══

PREP TIME: 25 minutes ★ **COOKING TIME:** 40 minutes ★ **YIELD:** 6 bombs

BISCUITS

2½ cups flour (measured after sifting)

1½ teaspoons baking powder

1½ teaspoons kosher salt

⅓ cup lard, cold (or ⅓ cup and 2 tablespoons butter)

¾ cup buttermilk

FILLING

½ cup Shredded Buffalo Chicken (page 101)

3 tablespoons Homemade Blue Cheese Dressing (page 38)

½ cup shredded mozzarella

3 tablespoons crumbled blue cheese

3 tablespoons softened cream cheese

⅓ cup Frank's RedHot Sauce

6 slices bacon

1. Place flour, baking powder, and salt in a mixing bowl and blend thoroughly.

2. Divide lard (or butter) in two portions. Add one to flour mixture and, working as fast as you can, mix in until lard disappears and flour becomes sandy. (If using stand mixer, blend on low 3 minutes.)

3. Break off nickel-sized portions of remaining lard and add to dough. Add buttermilk and stir a few times to combine.

4. Roll dough out a ½ inch thick. Use a cookie cutter to portion out six biscuits. (Combine scraps if needed). Cover tightly in plastic wrap and chill in fridge.

5. Prepare Shredded Buffalo Chicken.

6. Preheat oven to 375°F.

7. In a bowl, add Buffalo Shredded Chicken, Blue Cheese Dressing, mozzarella, blue cheese, and cream cheese. Mix thoroughly.

8. Use a rolling pin to roll biscuit dough rounds out ¼ inch thick.

9. Scoop 1½ tablespoons filling into center of each round. Drizzle 1 tablespoon hot sauce on top of filling, pull sides up around the filling and pinch closed to seal. Wrap bacon slice around each biscuit bomb, using it to cover the seam.

10. Place bombs in a cast-iron skillet so they are not touching.

11. Bake 25 minutes. Serve (with a warning) straight from oven.

Pro-Tip: The original recipe for Edna's biscuits calls for homemade baking powder. Did you even know you could make it yourself or are you still using that same open box you've been keeping in the back of the fridge the past three years to eliminate stray smells? Just mix ¼ cup cream of tartar with 2 tablespoons baking soda. According to Peacock, the idea behind making your own is that it doesn't have the metallic ting that comes with using powders made with aluminum sulfate–based powders. If you're making Tom & Jerrys you already have the cream of tartar.

DEVILISHLY BUFFALO

You *could* really go wild, tricking out deviled eggs Buffalo-style. Cook up a chicken breast, chop it fine, fine, fine, toss it in wing sauce and either toss it in with the yolk mixture or use to top the eggs. Brush some chicken skin with wing sauce, flatten it out on some parchment paper, bake it for an hour at 350°F, then chop the crispy skin up and use it as garnish atop the deviled eggs to echo the crispiness of a wing. You could also go *heavy* with the blue cheese in the yolk mixture. I don't know though—for me, there's just something a little weird about combining the chicken meat with yolk *inside* the egg whites—which came first, chicken or egg, all mixed up together in such close quarters. This is one of those cases where you're better off letting the egg stand in for the chicken and introducing all of Buffalo wings' flavors and accompaniments into the mix.

BLUE CHEESE BUFFALO DEVILED EGGS

PREP TIME: 25 minutes ★ **COOKING TIME:** 10 minutes ★ **YIELD:** 12 deviled egg halves

8 large eggs

2 teaspoons mayonnaise (for homemade, page 100)

1 tablespoon sour cream

2 teaspoons Frank's RedHot Sauce

½ teaspoon lemon juice

2½ tablespoons crumbled blue cheese

⅛ teaspoon celery salt

⅛ teaspoon white pepper

⅛ teaspoon mustard powder

1 tablespoon finely chopped or julienned fresh parsley

¼ teaspoon cayenne

1 tablespoon peeled and minced celery (leaves reserved for garnish)

1 tablespoon peeled and minced carrot

1 tablespoon crumbled Buffalo-ized Bacon (page 97, optional)

1 small serrano pepper, very thinly sliced

continued

1. Bring a large pan of water to a boil over high heat. Cautiously lower eggs into water with a slotted spoon, then lower heat to maintain a gentle boil for 10 minutes. Remove eggs to an ice bath and cool until barely warm (2 to 3 minutes).

2. Peel eggs fat-end first, rinse, and slice in half lengthwise. Carefully remove the yolks to a bowl without breaking the whites. Choose the twelve nicest looking egg-white halves.

3. In a bowl, combine yolks, mayo, sour cream, ¼ cup hot sauce, lemon juice, 2 tablespoons blue cheese, celery salt,

pepper, mustard, parsley, and half the cayenne. Mash yolks and mix thoroughly until smooth and evenly combined. Stir in minced celery, and carrots.

4. Collect mixture to one corner of a large sealable plastic bag. Cut off the tip of the corner and pipe mixture into hard-boiled egg whites.

5. Garnish each Buffalo deviled egg with remaining cayenne and blue cheese, and top each with a celery leaf, an optional crumble of bacon, a few drops of Frank's, and (for the heat-seekers) a thin slice of serrano.

PIMPED OUT BUFFALO SHRIMP

The rock shrimp tempura, made famous in New York City in the '90s by Chef Nobu Matsuhisa, is creamy, crunchy, and addictive. Believe it or not, blue cheese, hot sauce, and jalapeño might be this dish's long-lost relatives. They add extra creaminess and a little sting.

BUFFALO ROCK SHRIMP WITH BLUE CHEESE TEMPURA

PREP TIME: 35 minutes ★ **COOKING TIME:** 8 minutes ★ **SERVES:** 2 people

SAUCE

Vegetable oil

¼ cup sesame oil

1 cup mayonnaise, preferably homemade (page 100) or Kewpie

6 tablespoons Frank's RedHot Sauce

SHRIMP TEMPURA

2 egg yolks

1¾ cups cold water

¼ cup ice cubes

2 cups cake flour

2 cups crumbled blue cheese

½ cup rice flour

1 pound rock shrimp

GARNISH

2 stalks celery, peeled and sliced thin

1 large carrot, peeled and sliced thin

2 tablespoons lemon juice

1 jalapeño, sliced thin

4 tablespoons tobiko (optional)

1. Preheat vegetable oil in fryer to 360°F (or fill a high-edged pot or skillet with enough vegetable oil to cover a batch of five shrimp). Then add sesame oil.

2. For the sauce: Thoroughly mix mayo and hot sauce. Set aside.

3. For the tempura batter: Combine yolks with ice cold water. Add ice cubes. Add 2 cups of flour all at once. Using chopsticks or a fork, combine gently, for 1 minute. Crumble 1½ cups blue cheese into the batter.

4. Set up a frying station near your fryer or pot of oil. Fill a plate or tray with rice flour. Place a bowl of batter next to it, and a paper towel–lined tray as the last stop for the cooked shrimp before you serve them.

5. Once the oil reaches 360°F, fry in batches of about five shrimps at a time, being careful not to crowd them. First, toss each shrimp in flour to coat on all sides. Then, using tongs or chopsticks, dunk shrimp in the batter and drop gently in the oil. Repeat until one batch is frying. Fry each batch 2 minutes, drain, then remove to paper towels to dry.

continued

6. Quickly toss shrimp in spicy mayo, then pile on serving plate. Garnish with carrot and celery shavings, a drizzle of lemon juice, some crumbled blue cheese, jalapeño slices, and optional tobiko, then serve.

POTSTICK-TO-YOUR-RIB-ERS

You really could run through this book's table of contents and check off a bunch of things that could equally fulfill the potential of being the perfect Buffalo potstickers. Leftover Beef on Weck finely chopped and topped with a dollop of horseradish-spiked sour cream, or a shallow, hot pool of au jus? Check. Thin dumplings filled with shredded chicken and dressed with Red Sox Sauce? Yup. Sealed pockets of diced stuffed banana peppers served in a light tomato sauce? Mmm. Minced Utica greens tucked inside and set adrift in a pool of riggie sauce? Oh, boy. How about a teaspoon of leftover Buffalo Queso (what's *leftover* queso?) that gushes out into a bowl of classic wing sauce paired with Buffalo sloppy joe meat—like a brazen Buffalo cousin of Afghani aushak—bizarre but delicious. Steamed? Fried? Sautéed in butter?

They're all winning combinations. But here's a combination worth starting with above all: Buffalo Chicken Pimento Cheese Salad served with Home-made Blue Cheese Dressing or a side of Blue Cheese Sour Cream. The melty cheese–soaked, carrot- and celery-studded shredded chicken spills out, spicy and speckled with jalapeño and pimento into a light, creamy sauce—zippy, tangy, and more powerful than you'd imagine these delicate potstickers could be.

Two things before you get started. There's a time and a place for making things from scratch. The time and equipment it takes to make your own pasta that's as thin as wonton wrappers? Not worth it. You should be able to find the small round wonton wrappers at your nearest grocery or specialty food market. If this is your first time making dumplings, here are two ways to shape them. First, moisten the edge along one half of the wrapper with a wet fin-ger or brush and spoon 1 to 2 teaspoons filling in the center. Then choose one of the following fold-ing methods:

Crescent fold: Place the top edge between index finger and thumb. Create a fold as you use your other fingers to pinch it closed. Repeat until there are 5 to 6 folds. Squeeze edges together to seal tightly.

Hat fold: Fold in half and seal tightly by pinching the edges together. Moisten one of the ends, bring both together, pinch, and seal. Rotate and pinch the edges to make sure it's sealed. The dumpling should resemble a little hat.

BUFFALO POTSTICKERS

PREP TIME: 1 hour ★ **COOKING TIME:** 20 to 30 minutes ★ **YIELD:** About 30 potstickers

½ to 1 cup Buffalo Chicken Pimento Cheese Salad (page 151)

30 to 36 small, round wonton wrappers

1 cup Homemade Blue Cheese Dressing (page 38) or Blue Cheese Sour Cream (page 95)

1. Prepare Buffalo chicken pimento cheese salad.

2. Fill and seal potstickers using either the crescent or hat folds.

3. Prepare blue cheese dressing or blue cheese sour cream.

4. To boil: Fill a large pot two-thirds full with water, cover, and bring to a boil over high heat. Add eight to ten dumplings (however many fit forming one layer). Cook 2 minutes more after they start to float. Remove with a strainer, drain, and serve. Repeat until they're all cooked.

5. To steam: Line steamer with parchment paper or cabbage leaves over 1 cup water. Cover and bring water to a boil. Steam dumplings until cooked through (about 3 to 5 minutes).

6. To pan-fry: Warm a large non-stick skillet over medium heat. Add 2 tablespoons vegetable oil and wait for it to shimmer. Add six to eight potstickers in one layer. Cook 1 minute. Then swirl them around in the skillet 2 minutes without flipping to form a golden-brown crust. Raise to high heat. Add enough water to cover a third of the potstickers. Cover and cook 3 minutes. Remove lid and cook until remaining water evaporates and golden-brown crust is crispy.

7. Serve potstickers with Blue Cheese Sour Cream or Blue Cheese Dressing.

YOU SHOULDA PUT A CHEESY BUFFALO CHICKEN RING ON IT

At its most basic, this recipe calls for cream cheese, mozzarella, chicken, hot sauce, and crescent rolls. If you imagine a Buffalo-ized stromboli from your favorite pizzeria, you get the idea. But it's a really fun one to riff on. (If you're not afraid of a little heat, try adding some chopped jalapeños or poblanos to the mix.) This recipe goes further, integrating *all* the traditional wing accompaniments into the mix, adding both sauces for dipping, and topping the ring with a little extra panache: some more cheese. Because why wouldn't you? Making your own crescent roll dough from scratch isn't hard, but part of what makes this viral Internet recipe work is the precut triangular *shape* of the store-bought stuff. If you're making crescent rolls from scratch, you're doing it wrong.

CHEESY BUFFALO CHICKEN RING

PREP TIME: 15 minutes ★ **COOKING TIME:** 30 minutes ★ **SERVES:** 8 to 12 people

1 cup cream cheese

2 cups Shredded Buffalo Chicken (page 101)

½ cup finely diced celery

½ cup finely diced onion

¼ cup scallions

¼ cup finely chopped parsley

1 cup Monterey Jack cheese

2 cups mozzarella

⅓ cup crumbled blue cheese

Freshly ground black pepper

Two 8-ounce cans crescent rolls

¼ cup Frank's RedHot Sauce

8 slices mozzarella

1 cup Buffalo Wing Sauce (page 22)

1 cup Homemade Blue Cheese Dressing (page 38)

1. Preheat oven to 375°F.

2. In a large bowl, mix cream cheese, Shredded Buffalo Chicken, celery, onion, scallions, parsley, Monterey Jack, blue cheese, and black pepper.

3. To better estimate the size of the ring, place a bowl large enough to hold 1 cup blue cheese dressing in the center of cookie sheet (about 4 to 5 inches).

4. Unroll crescent roll triangles and arrange them around the bowl in a circle to resemble sunrays, fat side closest to the bowl in the center.

5. Evenly scatter 1 cup mozzarella on the dough closest to the center (about 1 to 2 inches). Drizzle ¼ cup hot sauce over mozzarella. Top with a layer of shredded chicken and cheese mixture. Cover with remaining cup of mozzarella.

6. Pull dough points up and over the chicken and cheese layers, tuck under

dough at the center and press together gently to seal.

7. Brush top of the chicken ring with ⅓ cup wing sauce. Remove the bowl from the cookie sheet.

8. Bake for 25 minutes. If you want to go over the top, drape mozzarella slices over

the top around the ring. Bake for another 5 minutes.

9. Slide onto serving plate, slice, and serve with a bowl of Blue Cheese Dressing in the center and Buffalo Wing Sauce on the side for dipping.

TWICE-BAKED, AND BUFFALOED

Potatoes obviously have nothing to do with the original Buffalo wings recipe, but they make a fantastic vehicle for their flavor. No surprise given that blue cheese, hot sauce, and sour cream—cornerstones of what make wings so great—also have a pretty fabulous track record with potatoes. This recipe adds richness to a dish that's typically already somewhat over-the-top by adding blue cheese and Cheddar to the mashed potato filling. And for those who like bacon bits . . . Buffalo bacon!

TWICE-BAKED BUFFALO WING POTATOES

PREP TIME: 45 minutes ★ **COOKING TIME:** 1 hour and 45 minutes ★ **YIELD:** 8 boats

4 potatoes

2 tablespoons vegetable oil

Kosher salt

1 cup Buffalo Wing Sauce (page 22)

1 cup Blue Cheese Sour Cream (page 95)

½ cup crumbled Buffalo-ized Bacon (page 97, optional)

½ cup butter

¾ cup heavy cream

1 cup shredded Cheddar

1 cup crumbled Saint Agur Blue

1 cup Frank's RedHot Sauce

16 Old-School Buffalo Wings (page 23)

1 carrot, thinly sliced

1 celery stick, thinly sliced

1. Preheat oven to 400°F.

2. Rub oil all over potatoes and season with salt. Bake 1 hour, then remove and let cool.

3. Prepare Buffalo Wing Sauce, Blue Cheese Sour Cream, and optional Buffalo-ized Bacon.

4. Slice potatoes lengthwise, being careful not to tear skin. Empty potato boats halves (reserving removed potato), hollowing close to the edge. Leave enough of the sides to maintain the structural integrity to hold up to all the good stuff you're about to pile in!

5. Use a ricer to finely mash reserved potatoes.

6. In a saucepan over medium heat, melt butter. Add heavy cream, bring to a rolling boil, then lower heat to simmer. Add riced potatoes, ⅓ cup Cheddar, ⅓ cup blue cheese, hot sauce, and 6 tablespoons Buffalo Wing Sauce. Stir to combine.

7. Fry wings (page 24) and let cool without saucing. Remove meat from the bones, roughly chop the chicken, and set aside.

8. Scatter a third of the remaining Cheddar evenly among the boat bottoms.

9. Scoop (or pipe) mashed potatoes evenly into each boat.

10. Toss chopped wing meat in wing sauce. Top each boat with the equivalent of two wings.

11. Scatter remaining Cheddar evenly over the boats and bake 20 minutes.

12. Scatter the thinly sliced celery and carrot over the top of each boat. Drizzle 1 teaspoon of Blue Cheese Sour Cream over each boat and crumble remaining blue cheese and optional Buffalo-ized Bacon on top and serve.

BUFFALO CHICKEN PARM "PIZZA" (PAGE 149)

ADDICTIVE BUFFALO-IZED PARTY DIPS & DISHES

◆———————◆

Like the original that inspired them, most of these dishes are indulgent, addictive, and really pretty messy. (In the cases of nachos, queso, sloppy joes, and 7-layer dip, maybe even messier.) And while they should all be an unqualified hit when hosting, the most impressive appearance-wise may be the nachos, which should be served on a baking sheet or cookie tray, and the chicken Parm pizza, which deserves (and actually needs) a pizza pan and can be sliced with a pizza cutter in front of guests for maximum effect. If that last one isn't a conversation starter ("Wait, the chicken *is* the pizza?"), I don't know what is.

These recipes are all mostly serve-yourself and friendly enough to be mostly made ahead of time. Consider preparing components of them (refried beans, shredded chicken, wing sauce, and blue cheese dressing for example) in advance, using a slow cooker to help keep others warm (queso and sloppy joes), and prepping things like the pimento cheese and coleslaw the night before. If you're looking for something pretty easy and delicious, the casserole can be prepared in about a half hour and only requires about 15 minutes of active cooking time. It can also be fancied up by using a ring mold to portion it out in individual servings that can then be warmed "to order" in the oven (rounds of it can even be portioned and frozen just up until the time you need them).

Most of these dishes *are* fairly straightforward and can be assembled by the seat of your pants for the first time for a party, but the chicken Parm pizza might not be one of them. If you don't plan on doing a dry run with it before serving it at the party, at least be sure to do the chicken prep the day before. You're going to want to give it a chance to fully set in the freezer.

LAKE EFFECT-ED DIP

I was surfing through recipes for "the most popular dips" and "the best Buffalo dips," and came across two links in particular that got me thinking. One was a layered Buffalo chicken dip by *How Sweet Eats* and the other was *Eater*'s post about the "right way" to make 7-layer dip. Buffalo chicken dip has to already be considered one of the top 10 all-time hall-of-famers next to artichoke and onion dips. But another of the greats *begs* Buffaloing (Buffalo-ization?): 7-layer dip.

As we all know, traditional 7-layer dip includes beans, cheese, guac, lettuce, sour cream, salsa, and olives. Now, many recipes call for a 1:1 ratio of these layers. *Eater*'s Sonia Chopra argues the beans are most important, with cheese a close second, and so there should be more of both than the other ingredients, and more beans than cheese. Now, personally I've never really understood how you can call lettuce or olives a "layer." Things that don't form an impervious layer don't deserve to be put in the same category as refried beans. (Shredded lettuce? Olives? "Layers?" Really?)

So after I was inspired to reinterpret a Nickel City approach to the dip, in the "more ain't enough" spirit of Buffalo's food scene, I was compelled to include seven *impenetrable* layers, including two layers of cheese and one layer of wing sauce (of course). Including ingredients like the lettuce and olive "layers" you'll find in a traditional 7-layer dip, this recipe has a baker's dozen—six of them garnish, in a thickness deep enough to count as the dip's "seventh layer." "Thirteen-layer dip" just doesn't sound as catchy, and hey, there's lake-effect snow in Buffalo! That 7-layer dip needs to bundle up in a few more layers.

One of the attractive things about this party appetizer has always been its toss-and-bake ease. This recipe does complicate things a little by asking you to make your own refried beans. It's a step you can *totally* skip (though you may want to doctor up your Old El Paso per the recipe). But the recipe for Buffalo Refried Beans included on page 99 is pretty much dump-and-stir (okay, dump, blend, and stir), and makes for a tasty dip of its own.

Two last things. You always want a glass dish when you make this dip (to show off the layers), but I always find the deep ones to be such a pain to effectively scoop top to bottom from so as to get some of everything on one chip. Instead, consider something longer and squat. And if you want to make this ahead, just leave off the scallions, celery, carrots, bacon, crumbled blue, and chopped parsley until you're ready to bake (or rewarm) and serve.

BUFFALO 7-LAYER DIP

PREP TIME: 35 minutes (using store-bought beans), 40 minutes (homemade beans) ★

COOKING TIME: 40 minutes (using store-bought beans) or 2 hours and 15 minutes (homemade beans) ★ **YIELD:** About 12 cups

1½ cups Buffalo Refried Beans (page 99)

If using store-bought beans:
¼ cup lard or vegetable oil
1 onion, chopped
4 cloves garlic, minced
One 4-ounce can pickled chiles or jalapeños
One 16-ounce can refried beans

9 slices Buffalo-ized Bacon, crumbled
2 cups shredded provolone
12 ounces cream cheese, whipped (Temp Tee brand, if you can find it)
⅓ cup Homemade Blue Cheese Dressing (page 38)
4 to 5 cups Shredded Buffalo Chicken (page 107)
2 cups shredded Monterey Jack
1 cup Buffalo Wing Sauce (page 22)
1 cup Blue Cheese Sour Cream (page 95)
4 scallions, diced
2 celery stalks, finely diced
2 carrot sticks, peeled and finely diced (optional)
1 cup crumbled Saint Agur Blue
½ cup finely chopped parsley
Tortilla chips
Celery and carrot sticks

1. Preheat oven to 400°F.

2. Prepare Buffalo Refried Beans or use your favorite store-bought version. If you're using store-bought, warm a pot over medium heat, melt lard, then cook onions 2 minutes. Add garlic and cook 2 more minutes. Add pickled chiles (and juice) and cook 2 more minutes. Add beans and mix well.

3. Prepare Buffalo-ized Bacon (or cook five slices bacon) and crumble.

4. Spread refried beans evenly over the bottom of a baking dish (preferably glass).

5. Top with shredded provolone.

6. Mix cream cheese with Blue Cheese Dressing. Spread evenly over the provolone.

7. Evenly cover cream cheese with Shredded Buffalo Chicken.

8. Cover with Monterey Jack, then cover cheese with Buffalo Wing Sauce.

9. Bake until warmed through and cheese covering has melted (about 10 to 15 minutes).

10. Spread a layer of Blue Cheese Sour Cream on top.

11. Garnish with scallions, celery, optional carrots, bacon, blue cheese, and parsley.

12. Serve hot, warm, or room temperature with tortilla chips and celery and carrot sticks.

CUE THE CASSEROLE

One of the reasons Buffalo wings are so beloved is the elemental aspect of the cooking process: fry wings, toss in sauce, eat. Sure, there are a few more steps involved—at the least, you have to melt the butter, cut the celery sticks, and pour the dressing—but as long as you cook them long enough, unless you want to complicate things to really differentiate them, it is what it is.

Casseroles can be similarly simple *and* easy to (over)complicate. By definition, a casserole is a one-dish, oven-baked meal that transforms ingredients that are greater as a sum of its parts. With core starches that include pasta, rice, potatoes, and cohesive elements that range from condensed soup to more cheese than you should be eating, it's a dish that can look and mean something different to you depending on who your people are and where you're from.

My aunt's broccoli cheese casserole is my all-time favorite. Outside that, for some reason, it's not a casserole to me without cheese and potatoes, preferably hash browns. This has both of those along with moist chunks of tender Buffalo chicken, a crunchy top, and creamy, zippy bite after bites-lurking underneath.

BUFFALO CHICKEN CASSEROLE

PREP TIME: 35 minutes ★ **COOKING TIME:** 1 hour and 20 minutes
(about 15 active) ★ **YIELD:** About 8 cups

One 30-ounce package hash browns, thawed

9 slices Buffalo-ized Bacon (page 97) or
    regular bacon, crumbled

1 cup Buffalo Wing Sauce (page 22)

2 chicken breasts, cut in ½-inch cubes

2 cups shredded Cheddar

3 tablespoons butter

1 onion, diced

2 cloves garlic, minced

1 cup minced celery

4 ounces canned pickled green chiles (or
    jalapeños), diced, liquid reserved

1 cup sour cream

1 cup chopped scallions

1¼ cups Homemade Blue Cheese Dressing
    (page 38)

1. Preheat oven to 400°F and be sure to thaw the hash browns.

2. Prepare Buffalo-ized Bacon or cook off some regular bacon and crumble.

3. Prepare Buffalo Wing Sauce.

4. Toss cubed chicken in a third of the wing sauce. Line a cookie tray with foil, toss chicken on the tray and bake 30 minutes.

5. Mix hash browns, cheese, and crumbled bacon. Reserve 1 cup of the mixture to the side.

6. In a large saucepan over medium heat, melt butter, then add onion, garlic, celery,

and chiles. Cook 3 minutes, then lower heat. Cook 10 minutes, until all liquid cooks out, but don't allow mixture to brown.

7. Remove onion mixture from heat and in a bowl, mix with sour cream and cheese-hash brown mixture.

8. Remove chicken from oven. Pour any liquid that pooled during roasting and add it and the reserved chile liquid to onion mixture over medium heat. Simmer until liquid evaporates (about 5 minutes).

9. Toss cooked chicken cubes with a third of the wing sauce, and combine chicken

and marinade thoroughly with the cheese-hash brown-onion-chile mixture.

10. Use butter (or cooking spray) to grease bottom and sides of casserole dish. Fill dish with mixture. Scatter reserved mixture of hash browns, cheese, and bacon evenly over the top.

11. Bake in oven 30 minutes, or until lightly browned.

12. Rest 5 minutes, then garnish with scallions and bacon. Serve drizzled with the remaining third of Buffalo Wing Sauce and Blue Cheese Dressing.

NA-CHO AVERAGE BUFFALO NACHOS

At least according to their lore, nachos, like wings, were born out of the unexpected arrival of a large, hungry party. In 1943 (about twenty years before wings were invented), a group of US Army wives walked into the Victory Club in Piedras Negras, Mexico, a restaurant in a border town across the Rio Grande River from Eagle Pass Army Airfield. Unable to find the chef, maître d' Ignacio "Nacho" Anaya supposedly surveyed the kitchen and cobbled together "Nachos Especiales," a plate of tortilla chips, cheese, and jalapeños.

Heat, cheese, and crunch are the major themes of both dishes, so great origin stories are far from the only reasons to pair them. And Buffalo-izing nachos results in an obvious win.

Just remember that there are two sins when it comes to nachos: insufficient ingredient coverage and sog. You either need to individually dress each chip or make sure there are enough toppings when you reach chips at the bottom. The problem is, if you pile on too much too early, those chips, the ones you get to toward the end, can get soggy.

One solution is to use a large, wide serving platter and to only go with one or two chip layers. Other things you can do? Trick out the nachos with lots of dry extras, like sliced olives and pickled jalapeños. And serve them with sides of the wet ingredients (refried beans, guac, queso, sour cream) in the center of the platter. For a creamy cheese sauce, sub out (or supplement) shredded cheese for Buffalo Queso (page 152).

Whatever you do, when it comes to toppings, don't be shy. And don't leave those tortilla chips high and dry.

BUFFALO CHICKEN NACHOS

PREP TIME: 45 minutes ★ **COOKING TIME:** 2 hours and 20 minutes
(20 minutes for the nachos) ★ **SERVES:** 4 to 8 people

6 cups Buffalo Refried Beans (page 99)

4 to 5 cups Buffalo Shredded Chicken (page 101)

4 cups shredded Cheddar

4 cups shredded Monterey Jack

4 onions, chopped

4 celery stalks, peeled and finely diced

Two 6-ounce cans black olives, sliced

2 large jalapeños (or ½ cup pickled jalapeños, drained), sliced thin

Two 14.5-ounce bags tortilla chips

2 cups Buffalo Queso (without the chicken, page 152)

1 cup Blue Cheese Sour Cream (page 95)

1 cup Buffalo Wing Sauce (page 22)

½ cup cotija

½ cup crumbled blue cheese

4 radishes, thinly sliced

2 large tomatoes, chopped

2 whole avocados, pitted and diced

2 limes, halved and quartered

1 cup cilantro, cleaned, destemmed, and chopped

1. Prepare Buffalo Refried Beans.

2. Prepare Shredded Buffalo Chicken.

3. Preheat oven to 500°F.

4. In one bowl, combine Cheddar and Monterey Jack cheeses. In another, combine garnish mixture by tossing onions, celery, black olives, and jalapenos.

5. Create a single, even layer of chips in a sheet tray.

6. Evenly scatter 2 cups of mixed cheese over the chips.

7. Use half of both the chicken and beans to create a roughly even layer of both over the cheese layer.

8. Evenly scatter a third of the garnish mix over the chicken and beans.

9. Evenly scatter 3 cups of cheese over the garnish.

10. Layer another even layer of chips on top.

11. Use remaining chicken and beans to create a roughly even layer of both over the chips.

12. Evenly scatter a third of the garnish over the chicken and beans.

13. Evenly scatter remaining cheese over the garnish.

14. Place sheet tray in oven and bake 20 minutes (until all the cheese has melted).

15. Remove nachos from oven. Drizzle Buffalo Queso over nachos, Blue Cheese Sour Cream over queso, and Buffalo Wing Sauce over sour cream.

16. Mix cotija and blue cheese. Evenly scatter remaining garnish, sliced radishes, chopped tomatoes, avocados, lime wedges, and cilantro on top. Serve.

BUFFALO ANOTHER LITTLE PIZZA MY PARM NOW, BABY

Michael Stillman's restaurant Quality Italian opened just blocks from Central Park in Manhattan in 2013, and quickly became famous for its chicken Parm "pizza" for two. It's an epic $68 dish invented by founding chefs Scott Tacinelli and Angie Rito where the "crust" is the actual chicken Parm, a forcemeat (puréed meat) made with breasts and thighs that have been fried and topped with sauce and cheese. That's right: the pizza isn't *topped* with chicken. It *is* chicken.

Walk through the dining room and you'll see it on every table.

In 2017, Tacinelli and Rito Buffalo-ized their signature dish as a takeout-only one-day special for Super Bowl Sunday (which they repeated for the Super Bowl in 2018). They swapped out the marinara for Buffalo sauce, added Muenster to their cheese blend and topped the pie with shaved celery and carrots, and a Gorgonzola buttermilk dressing. And wow, was it good. So good it *had* to be

included as an essential Buffalo chicken party dish. It's one of those dishes folks will always remember. And while there's a little prep involved, it's actually not hard to make.

Quality Italian does 13-inch "pizzas" but they have fryers big enough to fry them whole. We don't. There are a few workarounds. The first is to bake. But let's be real: it's not the same. The second? Fry but go smaller—say eight inches wide. That's easy. All you need is a deep pot at least 10 inches wide, and enough oil to cover the disc once it's in the pot. If you want to go that route, just halve this recipe.

If you want to make it as big as the restaurant does, follow this recipe. Just quarter the chicken disc before it's frozen through, then fry each quarter individually and reassemble them in your serving tray.

This calls for Buffalo Bread Crumbs (page 98) and Homemade Blue Cheese Dressing (page 38), but if you want to reduce prep time, just use your favorite store-bought Italian bread crumbs and blue cheese dressing. The only thing you shouldn't stray from is the mix of thigh and breast meat. You want the fat from that dark meat.

BUFFALO CHICKEN PARM "PIZZA"

PREP TIME: 5 hours and 5 minutes (65 minutes active) ★
COOKING TIME: 22 minutes ★ **SERVES:** 4 to 8

1½ pounds chicken breasts, chunked

1½ pounds chicken thighs (skinless and boneless), chunked

2 teaspoons dried oregano

2 teaspoons garlic powder

2 teaspoons onion powder

1½ teaspoons kosher salt

1½ teaspoons freshly ground black pepper

Vegetable or peanut oil

2 eggs

½ cup milk

1½ cups Buffalo Bread Crumbs (page 98)

½ cup plain bread crumbs

1 cup Wondra flour

1½ cups Buffalo Wing Sauce (½ cup reserved for dipping, page 22)

¼ cup sesame seeds (optional)

2 cups shredded Muenster

2 cups shredded mozzarella

1 cup Pecorino Romano

1 celery stalk, peeled and shaved

1 large carrot, peeled and shaved

1½ cups Homemade Blue Cheese Dressing (1 cup reserved for dipping, page 38)

⅓ cup honey (optional)

½ teaspoon red pepper flakes (optional)

1. Line a 14-inch pizza tray or pie plate with plastic wrap.

2. In a food processor or blender add chunked chicken, oregano, garlic, onion, salt, and pepper. Pulse until seasoning is thoroughly mixed and the chicken turns pasty (about 1 minute).

3. Press chicken mixture into plastic-lined tray evenly out to the edges until the surface is flat and about ⅓ inch thick. Cover with plastic wrap and freeze 4 hours. (If you're going 13 to 14 inches wide, cut disc into quarters after 2 hours, then return to freezer for another 2 hours.)

4. Preheat fryer or fill a deep pot at least 10 inches wide with enough vegetable oil to cover the size of the disc (or its cut portions that you've chosen to make) to 350°F.

5. Whisk together eggs and milk. In another bowl, combine bread crumbs.

6. Set up a dredge station with three large trays big enough to hold the frozen chicken disc. Use the first tray for the Wondra, the second for the egg dredge, and the third for the bread crumbs.

7. Retrieve chicken disc from pan and discard plastic wrap. Coat both sides of the disc first in the flour, then the egg dredge, then the bread crumbs.

8. Fry chicken 3 minutes until golden brown and place it on a pizza tray with the

continued

point directed toward the center of the tray. Repeat until all the chicken has been fried and reassembled.

9. Preheat oven to 400°F.

10. Brush entire surface of disc evenly with Buffalo Wing Sauce.

11. Optional: Along the outer rim of the edge, scatter sesame seeds on the "crust" about a half an inch from the rim toward the center to form a sesame seed "pizza" crust.

12. Combine Muenster, mozzarella, and Pecorino Romano, then scatter evenly over the surface of the pizza, leaving the optional sesame crust uncovered.

13. Place the Buffalo Chicken Parm "Pizza" in the oven until the cheese has completely melted, about 10 minutes.

14. Scatter shaved celery and carrot, and drizzle blue cheese dressing evenly over the pizza so that there will be an even amount on every slice.

15. Use a pizza cutter to slice the pie into eight slices. If you've made the 14-inch pie by cutting it in quarters, note where the slices have been cut and slice each quarter in half.

16. Serve with Buffalo Wing Sauce and Blue Cheese Dressing for dipping. (Optional: Mix honey and chile flakes and offer for drizzling.)

PIMENTUFFALO? PIMUFFALO? PIMENTALO?

If you don't like pimento cheese, you probably just haven't had one made the right way yet. Pimento cheese is a southern staple, but Buffalo-izing it seems perfectly within rights, given its birthplace is actually said to be New York (Google it, and remember that Philadelphia appellation be damned, New York invented cream cheese too).

The essential players are simple: cheese, cream cheese, pimentos, and mayo—but this recipe adds shredded chicken, which makes for a chicken salad spread that doesn't require melting cheese, or toasted bread to make an excellent sandwich.

═══ BUFFALO CHICKEN PIMENTO CHEESE SALAD ═══

PREP TIME: 25 minutes ★ **COOKING TIME:** 15 minutes ★ **YIELD:** 3 to 4 cups

1 cup Shredded Buffalo Chicken (page 101)

½ cup softened cream cheese

5 tablespoons Frank's RedHot Sauce

One 7-ounce jar pimentos, drained and finely chopped

⅔ cups shredded Cheddar

2 tablespoons crumbled Saint Agur Blue

Pinch cayenne

6 tablespoons mayonnaise, preferably homemade (page 100) or Kewpie

½ celery, finely minced

½ carrot, shredded

¼ onion, finely minced

¼ jalapeño, finely minced

Crackers, toast points, or carrot and celery sticks

1. Prepare Buffalo Shredded Chicken, without sauce.

2. In a bowl, add cream cheese, hot sauce, pimentos, Cheddar, blue cheese, cayenne, and mayo. Mash with a fork or pulse in a food processor until fairly smooth (but not whipped).

3. Add celery, carrot, onion, jalapeño, and shredded chicken.

4. Toss until well combined.

5. Serve with your favorite crackers or toast points, or celery and carrot sticks, or melted into a grilled cheese (page 109).

BUFFALO QUESO? JUST SAY SO

Queso has to be one of the easiest and most delicious dips in the world. The more authentic version, made using poblanos, chorizo, and a Mexican melting cheese like Asadero, is amazing. But keep a close eye on any food snobs hovering near the party table when there's some straight-up Tex-Mex queso around—even those who turn their noses up at the *idea* of processed cheese will find it hard to resist.

Yes, there's something beautiful (and very '50s-esque) in the simple equation that uses two store-bought ingredients (one package of Velveeta to one can of Ro*Tel), warmed either in the microwave, in a crockpot, or on the stove, and served. As any good Texan will tell you, the slow cooker is the best friend to queso (and a hurried host), because it will keep it at the desired "Liquid Gold" consistency.

BUFFALO QUESO

PREP TIME: 5 minutes ★ **COOKING TIME:** 15 to 60 minutes ★ Yield: 5 cups

One 32-ounce package Velveeta, cubed
Two 10-ounce cans Ro*Tel Original Diced
    Tomatoes & Green Chilies
½ cup Buffalo Wing Sauce (page 22)
2 celery stalks, peeled and minced
1 carrot, peeled and minced
Tortilla chips
Celery and carrot sticks (optional)

1. If you're using a slow cooker, turn the setting to low, add cubed Velveeta, Ro*Tel, and Buffalo Wing Sauce, then cover. Cook until the cheese has completely melted (30 to 60 minutes). If cooking on the stovetop, add Velveeta, Ro*Tel, and Buffalo Wing Sauce to a large saucepan, and cook over medium heat for 15 minutes.

2. Add celery and carrot. Stir until completely combined.

3. Serve with tortilla chips, and/or celery and carrot sticks, if desired.

Voulez-Vous Poulet Mon Queso, Ce Soir?

To truly Buffalo-ize your queso, you need chicken. Try adding leftover rotisserie chicken, Shredded Buffalo Chicken (page 101), or cubed roast chicken breast. For the latter, preheat the oven to 400°F, toss cubed chicken in wing sauce and into a foil-lined cookie tray, then bake 30 minutes.

A MANWICH IS A MEAL, BUT A BUFFWICH IS THE REAL DEAL

According to the *Chicago Tribune*, you have a cook named Joe at a Sioux City, Iowa, cafe to thank for having invented the "loose meat sandwich" in 1930 that went on to be called the "Sloppy Joe." Traditionally, the version we know from school cafeterias is a saucy affair, usually sweetened with ketchup, given that "what's-that-flavor" accent with Worcestershire sauce, and liberally dusted with garlic, onion, mustard, and chili powders. Sometimes the rest of the spice cabinet, too.

But seeing that iconic 57 varieties brand on sloppy joes recipe ingredient lists begs the question: if ketchup, why not hot sauce? And if ground beef, why not ground chicken? If ground chicken and hot sauce, why not blue cheese to three-note a typically two-note dish (bun and meat). And if already messy, why not roll up your sleeves for some classic forearm drip and add dressing for better blue cheese distribution? The answers to these questions (albeit with a few optional wing element garnish touches) all lead to Buffalo chicken sloppy joes. Or as I like to call them, "Buffalo joes."

BUFFALO CHICKEN SLOPPY JOES (A.K.A. BUFFALO JOES)

PREP TIME: 35 minutes ★ **COOKING TIME:** 1 hour and 10 minutes ★ **YIELD:** 6 Buffwiches

6 tablespoons butter

1 pound ground chicken meat

Kosher salt

Freshly ground black pepper

1 small onion, finely diced

1 small cayenne pepper or jalapeño

3 cloves garlic, minced

3 celery stalks, finely diced

3 large carrots, peeled and shredded (or finely diced)

6 tablespoons Frank's RedHot Sauce

¼ cup ketchup

3 tablespoons Worcestershire sauce

1 cup Genesee beer (or your favorite beer)

1 cup chicken stock

2½ cups Homemade Blue Cheese Dressing (page 38)

1 cup Buffalo Wing Sauce (optional, page 22)

6 sesame-seeded rolls (or your favorite hamburger rolls)

12 slices provolone

½ cup Saint Agur Blue (or your favorite blue cheese)

1 dill pickle, finely diced

½ cup minced scallions

½ teaspoon celery seeds

1. Warm a large skillet over medium-high heat. Melt butter, then add ground chicken, salt, and pepper. Break up the meat with a wooden spoon and cook 6 minutes, stirring halfway through.

continued

2. Add onion, hot pepper, garlic, and ¾ of both diced celery and carrots. Reserve remaining celery and carrots for garnish. Cook 7 minutes.

3. Add Frank's, ketchup, Worcestershire, beer, and chicken stock. Stir well to thoroughly combine. Bring to a boil, then simmer until thick enough to spread on a roll (about 45 minutes). Add salt and pepper to taste.

4. Meanwhile, prepare Blue Cheese Dressing and optional Buffalo Wing Sauce.

5. Turn on the broiler. Slice open the rolls and place under the broiler until lightly toasted.

6. Remove rolls from oven and place three rolls each on two oven-safe plates or sizzle platters. Place slice of cheese on bottom buns, then ladle ½ cup Buffalo sloppy joe mixture on top of cheese on each bun. Top each with another slice of cheese.

7. Place sizzle platter under the broiler just long enough to melt the cheese.

8. Top each bottom half with crumbled blue cheese, diced pickle, scallions, and celery seeds.

9. Drizzle Blue Cheese Dressing and optional Buffalo Wing Sauce on top, cover with top buns, and serve.

WHAT YOU WANT WHEN YOU THINK "BUFFALO CHIP DIP"

There are at least three other dip recipes in this book (Buffalo Chicken Pimento Cheese Salad, page 151; Buffalo 7-Layer Dip, page 143; and Buffalo Queso, page 152), as well as recipe extra level-ups (blue cheese sour cream, onion, and shredded chicken dips). And am I wrong that there are several other mixtures used in other recipes that could easily be turned *into* dips? Blue Cheese Dressing, page 38, Blue Cheese Sour Cream, page 95, Red Sox Wing Sauce, page 45, and riggies sauce could easily be paired with potato chips. To say nothing of chopped stuffed banana peppers, Utica greens, chicken pot pie filling, and Buffalo casserole. All of those things could be repurposed as dips with one chip (or crudité) or another.

But the Duff's chicken wing dip that they seem to serve at every location *except* the original one in Amherst is the quintessential one you're looking for if you're trying to visualize "chicken wing dip." At least, after tasting it, that's all I can think of when I think of what a Buffalo chip dip should be. Duff's is made with their own hot sauce and blue cheese and served with "bottomless" tortilla chips. So after some experimentation (and some polite interrogation of my waitress) I've recreated a dip worth ordering with your wings if you're making a quick pit stop at the Depew location on the way in or out of town via Buffalo Niagara International Airport.

Of course, if you're lucky enough to live *in* Buffalo, there's only one sour cream you'd even dream of using: Bison ("Hang Out. Dip In."). And Bison's French Onion and Bacon French Onion Dips are legitimate stand-ins for sour cream in this recipe. If you don't, just use the richest one you can find. The shredded chicken recipe in this book is meant to be incorporated into this one, but rotisserie chicken or cooked cubed chicken breast works excellently too.

BUFFALO CHIP DIP

PREP TIME: 8 minutes ★ **COOKING TIME:** 20 minutes ★ **YIELD:** 5 cups

¾ cup shredded mozzarella

¾ cup shredded Cheddar

2 cups Shredded Buffalo Chicken (page 101)

½ cup Frank's RedHot Sauce

1½ cups room-temperature whipped cream cheese

1 cup sour cream

½ cup crumbled blue cheese

¼ cup minced celery

¼ cup minced carrots

½ onion, chopped

2 cloves garlic, pressed

4 cups tortilla chips

continued

1. Preheat oven to 425°F.

2. Mix mozzarella and Cheddar. Reserve ½ cup cheese.

3. Add all ingredients (except reserved cheese mixture and tortilla chips) to a large bowl or oven-safe baking dish.

Stir thoroughly to combine, about 3 to 5 minutes.

4. Bake 17 minutes. Evenly scatter reserved cheese to cover. Bake 3 to 5 minutes.

5. Serve with tortilla chips.

BUFFA-SLAW-SOME

Yeah, you can use slaw as a crisp, refreshing foil to a spicy picnic or barbecue dish. But the creamy mayo-vinegar base and the usual appearance of shredded carrots also makes it super receptive when it comes both to flavor and theme. To fully embrace the riff, consider skipping the mayo here and instead substituting it with 2/3 cup blue cheese dressing and doubling the cider vinegar (to 1/4 cup).

BUFFALO COLESLAW (BUFFASLAW)

PREP TIME: 20 minutes ★ **YIELD:** 8 cups

1 cup mayonnaise (for homemade, page 100)

3 tablespoons cider vinegar

1/4 cup Frank's RedHot Sauce

1/2 tablespoon honey

1 teaspoon celery seed

1 teaspoon kosher salt

1/4 teaspoon white pepper

2 cups shredded green cabbage, sliced very thinly

2 cups shredded purple cabbage, sliced very thinly

2 cups grated carrot

2 cups shredded celery, sliced very thinly

1/2 cup crumbled blue cheese

1 cup chopped chives

1. Whisk mayo, vinegar, hot sauce, honey, celery seed, kosher salt, and pepper in a large bowl.

2. Toss shredded cabbages, carrot, and celery with mayo mixture until completely coated.

3. Keep chilled until you serve, then garnish with blue cheese and chives.

A Sweet, Crunchy Touch: Try skipping the honey and instead adding peeled, cored honeycrisp or Fuji apples that you've julienned. It's a nice sweet contrast to the zip of the hot sauce.

DAYTRIP DISHES

According to at least one new St. Louis–based food festival, Flavored Nation, it's not bagels, pizza, or pastrami, but the chicken wing that's New York State's most iconic food. But New York state has many other unsung and celebrated food pilgrimages and creations.

Consider the following foods and their New York State birthplaces:

Jell-O, LeRoy

Potato Chips, Saratoga Springs

Shredded Wheat, Niagara Falls

Thousand Island Dressing, Clayton

Philadelphia Cream Cheese, Lowville

And that doesn't even get into the claim that the first hamburger in America was made at the Erie County Fair in Hamburg in 1885, *not* at Louis' Lunch in New Haven, Connecticut, in 1895.

Whether we're talking Rochester's garbage plate, Naples' grape pie, Binghamton's spiedies, Utica's eats triad (greens, riggies, and tomato pies), or Oneonta's Cornell chicken and cold cheese slice, Buffalo makes a great beginning or final destination on an epic food road trip across New York State.

Here are some recipes for recreating a few of the most iconic food daytrip musts outside Buffalo ranging from just over 75 minutes to four hours.

GETTIN' RIGGIE WITH IT

What is it about chicken, food creativity, and hazy origin stories? You have to wonder when delving into the birth of chicken riggies, a Utica rigatoni dish said to have originally been made with just cubed chicken, cherry peppers, wine, marinara, and cheese. If you've never had riggies, imagine a smooth, spicy sauce made with so much grated cheese that you'd think it was made with cream. It's tangy, silky, sweet, hot, and vinegary—one of those overindulgent, Italian-American dishes nowhere near "authentic" but too good to refuse.

Riggies is said to have been invented in 1979, at an Italian restaurant called Clinton House owned by Chef Richie Scamardo with Chef Bobby Hazleton. Chef Michael Geno, who worked there at the time, said it was invented in 1979. "The doctors, lawyers, and union guys would come in on Monday nights to play cards and we would make them the 'riggie dish' with chicken, tomatoes, and cherry peppers," he said. "When they came back the next week, they wanted the same thing we made them the week before. And there you have it—the birth of chicken riggies."

Today, there are as many versions as restaurants in Utica, and many have strayed from the initial recipe—adding onions, mushrooms, black olives, and garlic—and adding heavy cream to the sauce. But according to Utica's WIBX 950AM, the original relied on cheese (not cream, which would make it more like a vodka sauce) for its signature velvety texture.

This recipe mimics the preparation Chef Adam Spellman of the Chesterfield Restaurant shared with WIBX 950AM's Bill Keeler in 2015. You can add more hot cherry peppers and chile flakes if you live on the spicy side. Just remember, this dish is piled high. If you want to veer off-script, try these variations found around Utica. From there, pepperoni, meatballs—the sky's the limit. If you switch from chicken or shrimp to meatballs, steak, or other red meats, swap the white wine out for red wine. If loving chicken riggies is wrong, I don't want to eat rigatoni.

Mushrooms: Add 1 cup sliced white mushrooms before the onions and cook 3 to 5 minutes.

Black olives: Add ¼ cup sliced black olives with the crushed tomatoes.

Shrimp: Substitute 8 to 9 large shrimp for chicken, and cook just 1 to 2 minutes twice, tossing in between.

Sausage: Substitute ½ pound crumbled sausage for chicken and cook 4 minutes.

CHESTERFIELD–STYLE CHICKEN RIGGIES

PREP TIME: 20 minutes ★ **COOKING TIME:** 30 minutes ★ **SERVES:** 2 people

Kosher salt

1 chicken breast, cut in half-inch chunks

Freshly ground black pepper

5 tablespoons butter

1 tablespoon extra virgin olive oil

½ cup chopped red onion

½ cup chopped roasted red bell peppers

½ cup chopped roasted green peppers (green chiles or cubanelles work too)

½ cup chopped pickled hot cherry peppers

3 cloves garlic, minced

½ teaspoon red pepper flakes

1½ to 2 cups rigatoni (paccheri or mezze rigatoni)

½ cup white wine

1 cup crushed tomatoes (or your favorite jarred tomato sauce)

2 cups grated Romano cheese

4 to 8 fresh basil leaves, minced (or chiffonade)

2 teaspoons grated Romano cheese, for garnish

1. Bring water to a boil in a large pot over high heat, then salt water.

2. Toss chicken chunks with salt and freshly ground pepper.

3. Set a large saucepan on medium heat, then add 1 tablespoon butter and olive oil to the saucepan and cook 1 minute. Add chicken and cook 2 minutes. Then toss the chunks in the pan and cook another 2 minutes. Remove and reserve.

4. Return pan to medium heat. Add 4 tablespoons butter. When it melts, add onion and peppers, then cook until soft (about 3 minutes). Season with freshly ground pepper, add garlic and crushed red pepper, then cook 1 to 2 more minutes. Return chicken to pan.

5. Add rigatoni to boiling water and stir occasionally for 10 to 12 minutes until the pasta is al dente.

6. Meanwhile, add wine to deglaze the saucepan. Add 1 cup crushed tomatoes (or tomato sauce), and reduce by about half. Add grated cheese and mix thoroughly. Allow cheese to fully incorporate into the sauce.

7. Strain and toss rigatoni into saucepan. Toss pasta until completely covered and thoroughly mixed, then put in two large bowls, garnish with basil and grated cheese, and serve.

GREAT GRAPE PIE

Seeds, skins, and the seasonality of Concords have to be what have held back grape pie from national acclaim. It's hard to imagine why else this delicious, and otherwise easy-to-make pie has largely remained a local treat since Irene Bouchard started making it for the Redwood Restaurant in Naples, New York, in the 1970s. Bouchard had been running a bakery at home since the '50s, and had a shop across from the Redwood. At some point, the restaurant started selling Concord grape pies that were being eaten as quickly as they could make them. Al Hodges, the Redwood's owner, asked Bouchard if she'd help. At her peak, Bouchard was making 17,000-plus pies a year, 10,000 in the fall, when Concords are available!

The Grape Pie Queen passed away in 2015, at the age of 98. But her legacy lives on. Two spots, Cindy's and Monica's, have anchored Naples' grape pie production for decades. Monica Schenk said she started baking grape pies in 1983. She sells pies frozen and fresh (the fresh pie has a "floating top" put on after the cooked filling is placed inside). Monica also tops pies with graham cracker crumbs, oats, brown sugar, butter, and cinnamon, and sells jars of filling and bags of pie crust. She published her recipe on her website if you want to make one from scratch. "There's one thing I do, just one thing I don't tell people," Monica says.

For the filling, pinch the grapes to remove and reserve the skins, cook and press the pulp, toss the seeds, and add lemon juice and sugar. "The crust is just a good old Crisco recipe with not too much water, just enough to give a feel to it," Monica said, and it's cooked separately, because otherwise, she said, the crust doesn't get cooked enough.

Your favorite supermarket pie crust will lop an hour and a half off this recipe, with nobody who hasn't visited Naples, New York, the wiser. But if you're aiming for authenticity, there are only a few differences between published recipes for Monica and Irene's pies to know. Monica's calls for ⅔ cup of butter-flavored Crisco and ⅓ cup of ice water for her crust. Irene's calls for ⅔ cup of shortening, and eschews water for ½ cup of skim milk. Monica calls for par-baking the crust, while Irene calls for baking the crust and filling together (with a milk glaze on the top crust). Beyond that, the only difference is the thickener. Monica uses cornstarch and Irene uses tapioca.

This recipe marries elements of each (I'm just not a fan of artificial flavors). As for the *how* of eating, Monica said, most folks in Naples do it cold.

GRAPE PIE

PREP TIME: 2 hours ★ **COOKING TIME:** 40 minutes ★ **SERVES:** 6 to 8 people

CRUST

2 cups pastry flour

1 teaspoon kosher salt

½ cup Crisco shortening

½ cup butter, cubed then frozen

⅓ cup ice water

FILLING

5 cups stemmed Concord grapes

½ cup sugar

3 tablespoons cornstarch (or substitute 1 tablespoon tapioca pearls)

3 teaspoons lemon juice

1. Add flour, salt, Crisco, and butter cubes in a stand mixer bowl, then mix on a low speed until crumbly. Slowly add ice water until mixture forms a ball. (If you'd prefer not to use a stand mixer, follow the same method, adding ingredients to a large bowl and mixing by hand until the dough comes together.)

2. Divide pastry dough into two portions on a floured surface, flatten and wrap each in plastic. Put in the fridge for 1 hour.

3. Pinch grape ends to slip skins off the pulp. Reserve pulps and skins separately.

4. In a small pot over medium-high heat, cook pulp until it boils and softens (about 5 minutes). Push the pulp through a sieve to remove the seeds (discard the seeds).

5. Add the skins, sugar, cornstarch, and lemon juice to the pulp and mix until thoroughly combined.

6. Preheat oven to 400°F.

7. Roll out one disc of pastry dough on a floured surface, wrap flattened dough on top of rolling pin, then place in a 9-inch pie pan. Flatten and even at along the pan bottom and sides, and crimp edges if you'd like.

8. Line pie dough with parchment paper, fill with 3 to 4 cups dry beans, and cook 15 to 20 minutes until golden brown. Remove and reserve (and remove the beans for next time!).

9. Roll out remaining pastry dough on a floured surface. Fill pie shell with grape filling, top with pastry, crimp closed, create four slits in the center, and return to oven 15 to 20 minutes, until golden brown.

"BARBECUED BROILERS WITHOUT SAUCE ARE LIKE BREAD WITHOUT BUTTER"

He's more well-known today for having invented the chicken nugget, but if you eat barbecue chicken anywhere in New York state at a place that's been around for a few decades, it's likely the recipe used was, if not invented by, then at least influenced by Cornell professor Robert Baker. "Barbecued broilers without sauce are like bread without butter," he wrote along with the recipe published in 1950, in the Cornell Cooperative Extension Information Bulletin 862, that inspired both Buffalo's own Chiavetta's (from the Erie County Farm and Home Center in East Aurora during a farm bureau convention), and Oneonta's Brooks' House of BBQ.

It's a simple recipe, brushed (or as at Brook's, flicked) on every few minutes, but folks never saw chicken the same way again. If you don't have poultry seasoning, you can use rosemary, sage, thyme, marjoram, celery salt, or a mix of whatever you like. The original recipe calls for just a tablespoon of seasoning, but doubling the herbs really adds more flavor. This recipe will use up about a half of the sauce; you can keep whatever's left over for up to a few weeks in the fridge.

ROBERT BAKER–STYLE
CORNELL BARBECUE CHICKEN

PREP TIME: 20 minutes ★ **COOKING TIME:** 1 hour ★ **SERVES:** 4 people

1 egg

1 cup vegetable oil

2 cups cider vinegar

3 tablespoons kosher salt

2 tablespoon poultry seasoning

½ teaspoon freshly ground black pepper

Four 1-pound broiler halves

1. Prepare your charcoal. Use about ½ pound of briquets per broiler half. You'll want the flames to disappear before you put the chicken on.

2. Beat egg, then whisk in the oil until combined.

3. Add vinegar, salt, seasoning, and pepper, and stir until thoroughly mixed.

4. Brush all sides of the halves thoroughly with the sauce, then put them on the grill fire after flames are gone.

5. Turn halves every 5 minutes, basting each time. Cook for about an hour or until the meat is not red in the center.

GREENS WITH ENVY FOR UTICA

Most restaurants would kill to be at the center of one iconic dish like riggies. Somehow, with Utica greens, the Chesterfield Restaurant is in the middle of two. Like wings in Buffalo aren't Buffalo wings, these are just "greens," "fried greens," or greens named after the restaurant or chef making them. The dish is a little spicy, a little cheesy, a little crunchy—altogether, more than a few incentives to eat your bitter greens. Think escarole cooked with garlic, prosciutto, hot cherry peppers, Parmesan, and bread crumbs, and then topped with more cheese and bread crumbs, broiled, and topped with more grated cheese, for luck. Why not?

According to an interview given to the *New York Times* in 2017, Utica greens—sorry, "greens"—started being served at the Chesterfield in 1988 (a year before riggies), when Chef Joe Morelle put them on the menu. The dish, a riff on one Morelle had seen another chef make while working at a restaurant (now closed) called Grimaldi's, was a hit. And like the Chesterfield's other hit, riggies, greens can now be found in many area restaurants, sometimes with variations (adding ingredients like potatoes, artichoke hearts, mushrooms, broccoli, melted mozzarella, and marinara, and swapping salami for the prosciutto).

This is a super easy dish that requires only two steps you may be unfamiliar with. The first is to blanch the greens (boiling them for two minutes, then immediately stopping the cooking by dunking them in ice water). The second is to make an oreganata, a fancy word for bread crumbs toasted with oregano and Parmesan—which is also great on baked clams. Escarole can also be pretty dirty, so be sure to wash it thoroughly before you begin.

The broiler has to be one of the most underused, underappreciated tools in the home kitchen, which is funny, given it's one of the tools at your disposal most likely to add that restaurant effect you can never seem to replicate when trying to imitate melted, crusty dishes. Just be sure to use a pan that can take direct heat, and don't forget it's in there!

UTICA GREENS

PREP TIME: 22 minutes ★ **COOKING TIME:** 11 minutes ★ **YIELD:** About 2 cups

¾ cup extra virgin olive oil

1 cup bread crumbs

¼ cup minced fresh oregano

1¼ cups grated Parmigiano-Reggiano

1 to 2 heads escarole (about 1½ pounds), leaves separated and thoroughly cleaned

4 slices prosciutto, chopped

5 hot cherry peppers, stemmed (also toss ⅔ of the seeds) and chopped

4 large cloves garlic, minced

Kosher salt

Freshly ground black pepper

1. Bring a large pot of hot water to a boil over high heat. Pour a few cups of ice in a large bowl of cold water to create an ice bath for the greens.

2. Make the oreganata: Mix ½ cup olive oil, bread crumbs, oregano, and ½ cup Parmigiano-Reggiano in a bowl and mix until sandy in texture. Reserve.

3. Blanch greens until they wilt (no more than 2 minutes), then immediately submerge in an ice bath for 2 minutes. Drain, squeeze out as much moisture as possible, then chop in 1- to 2-inch pieces. Reserve.

4. Turn broiler on high and set a large saucepan on medium heat. Add 2 tablespoons olive oil, then sauté prosciutto, peppers, and garlic for 3 minutes. Add greens, season with salt and pepper, and mix well.

5. Add half of oreganata mixture and ½ cup Parmigiano-Reggiano to pan, stirring frequently and scraping the bottom for 3 minutes.

6. Cover thoroughly with remaining oreganata and place pan under broiler (or put the greens on a metal sizzle platter or serving platter) until bread crumbs are toasty brown and the cheese seems to have melted (2 to 3 minutes).

7. Drizzle with remaining olive oil, garnish with 2 to 4 tablespoons grated cheese, and serve.

ACKNOWLEDGMENTS

There are three people without whom this book would literally have not happened. Thank you to my agent Stacey Glick for having wanted to do a Buffalo-related cookbook for years and for channeling my enthusiasm to Countryman Press. Thanks to one of her other authors, Michelle Buffardi, author of *Great Balls of Cheese*, for being a vegetarian and asking my wife if a wing-related book would be something I'd be interested in working on.

Last of the three, and most important, thank you to my wife Angela Moore. Not just for bringing Buffalo adventures into my life and being supportive throughout the year I spent writing two books and for going solo for a month at home while I was away getting fat, but for enduring the months after our son Gus was born that *this book* still wasn't and for suffering through endless Buffalo-themed dinners (okay, that last part was actually delicious and not hard at all). I love you. Thank you for everything. I love you.

Thank you to my parents Rosmarie and Arthur Bovino for doing read-throughs and for always believing in me, and to my sister Emily for advice on all things authentic Italian.

Thank you to our friend Deb Perelman of *Smitten Kitchen* for patiently answering questions about photography and other how-to details that came up in the course of trying to write a cookbook, and for suggesting a few really fun recipe ideas that should have been included from the start.

Thank you to all the writers, chefs, pizzaiolos, restaurateurs, bloggers, and bartenders I interviewed during the month I spent eating and drinking my way through Buffalo, and hassled afterward with endless questions. In particular, Donnie Burtless of *Buffalo Eats*, my anonymous pizza paesano Sexy Slices who reviews the city's pizza in anonymity, and above all, Christa Glennie Seychew, who was generous with her time *in* Buffalo but also thoughtfully responded to all of my questions, emails, and texts about the inane, arcane, minute, and crucial details of all things Buffalo, food-related and not.

Thank you to Visit Buffalo Niagara and its Communications Manager Brian Hayden for answering questions and providing some logistics and support. Thanks to its Marketing Manager Drew Drown and his fiancée (now wife!) Bernice Radle for hosting me, giving me some great tips on places to hit, letting me keep pizza in their freezer, and not telling me I could never come back after leaving much of it there.

Thank you to Countryman Press, specifically editorial director Ann Treistman, my copyeditor Jenny Gropp, and production manager Devon Zahn. And thank you to my senior editor Róisín Cameron for her patience and dedication.

Thank you to my former *New York Times* bunker mate and boss Dan Okrent (public editor #1) for making some fun connections, and Colman Andrews for always seeming to know the answer to arcane food questions and connecting me to people who could answer the rare questions you couldn't. Thank you to my former word people at *Mouth .com*, Nancy Cohen, Jenny Acosta, Kaitlin Orr, and Josie Adams. If I hadn't worked with you, this book would not have been as punny. Any good puns I'll attribute to you. The bad ones are my fault.

Thank you to Barak Zimmerman for a long walk in April that helped dislodge the words. Once they started, they wouldn't stop.

Lastly, thank you to the city of Buffalo and everyone there who bought me a drink and welcomed me with open arms.

INDEX

Note: Page references in *italics* indicate photographs.

A

Abigail's (Waterloo), 18, 32–33
Anchor Bar (Buffalo), 17, 22
Andrés, José, 31
Andrzejewski, Mike, 71
Ayres, Jenn, 112–13

B

Bacon
  Buffalo Chicken Biscuit Bombs, 129–31
  Buffalo Chicken Casserole, 144–45, *145*
  Buffalo Fried Rice, *115,* 115–16
  Buffalo-ized, *96,* 96–97
  Buffalo 7-Layer Dip, 143
  Buffalo Wedge Salad, *120,* 120–21
  Twice-Baked Buffalo Wing Potatoes, *137,* 137–39
Baker, Robert, 164
Bar Bill Tavern (East Aurora), 18, 49
Bases Loaded (Blasdell), 18–19, 44
The Bazaar (Los Angeles and Miami), 31
Beans
  Buffalo Chicken Nachos, 146–47
  Buffalo 7-Layer Dip, 143
  Refried Buffalo, 99
Beef
  Buffalo Stinger Taco, 81–84, *82*
  on weck, about, 56–57
  on Weck, Easy, 53–54, *55*
  on Weck Roast Beef, *48,* 51–52
Bellissimo, Teressa, 17, 22
Billitier, Lou, 79
Biscuit Bombs, Buffalo Chicken Bacon, 129–31

Blake, Adam, 36
Blue Cheese
  Broccoli and Cauliflower "Wings," 127–29, *129*
  Buffalo Chicken Casserole, 144–45, *145*
  Buffalo Chicken Parm "Pizza," 147–50, *148*
  Buffalo Chicken Pot Pie, *110,* 110–12
  Buffalo Chicken Sloppy Joes (A.K.A. Buffalo Joes), 153–54, *154*
  Buffalo Chip Dip, 155–56, *156*
  Buffalo Coleslaw (Buffaslaw), 157
  Buffalo Deviled Eggs, 131–32, *132*
  Buffalo Potstickers, 134–35
  Buffalo Sauce, Spicy, 46
  Buffalo Stinger Taco, 81–84, *82*
  Buffalo Wedge Salad, *120,* 120–21
  and Buffalo Wings Buttermilk Waffles, 105–8, *106*
  Chef Marshal Grady's Bleu Bayou Wings, *32,* 32–34
  Cream of Buffalo Wing Soup, 124–25, *125*
  Dressing (For Wings), Homemade, 37–39, *38*
  Primanti Sandwich, Buffalo-Style, 121–23
  Sour Cream, 95–96
  Speed Metal Fries, 112–14
  Stuffed Banana Peppers, 84–86, *85*
  Tempura, Buffalo Rock Shrimp with, 133–34, *134*
  Twice-Baked Buffalo Wing Potatoes, *137,* 137–39
Bologna
  Fried, Sandwich, *67,* 67–68
  popularity of, 66–67

Bouchard, Irene, 162

Bread Crumbs
    Buffalo, 98
    Buffalo Panko, 98

Bread(s)
    Homemade Kummelweck Rolls, 49–50, *51*
    Oliver's Spinach Loaf, 71–73, *72*

Broccoli and Cauliflower "Wings," 127–29, *129*

Buffalo cuisine
    famous wing spots, 18–21
    history and timeline, 14–15
    other iconic dishes, 59

C

Cabbage
    Buffalo Coleslaw (Buffaslaw), 157
    Primanti Sandwich, Buffalo-Style, 121–23

Candy, Sponge, *89,* 89–91

Caraway seeds
    Easy Beef on Weck, 53–54, *55*
    Homemade Kummelweck Rolls, 49–50, *51*

Carrots
    Baked Buffalo Wings, 28–30, *30*
    Buffalo Coleslaw (Buffaslaw), 157
    Buffalo Fried Rice, *115,* 115–16
    Cream of Buffalo Wing Soup, 124–25, *125*
    Old-School Buffalo Wings, 23–24

Cauliflower and Broccoli "Wings," 127–29, *129*

Celery
    Baked Buffalo Wings, 28–30, *30*
    Broccoli and Cauliflower "Wings," 127–29, *129*
    Buffalo Coleslaw (Buffaslaw), 157
    Buffalo Fried Rice, *115,* 115–16
    Chef Marshal Grady's Bleu Bayou Wings, *32,* 32–34
    Cream of Buffalo Wing Soup, 124–25, *125*
    Old-School Buffalo Wings, 23–24

Charlie the Butcher, 51, 56–57

Cheese. *See also* Blue Cheese
    Buffalo Chicken Bacon Biscuit Bombs, 129–31
    Buffalo Chicken Casserole, 144–45, *145*
    Buffalo Chicken Nachos, 146–47
    Buffalo Chicken Parm "Pizza," 147–50, *148*
    Buffalo Chicken Pot Pie, *110,* 110–12
    Buffalo Chicken Sloppy Joes (A.K.A. Buffalo Joes), 153–54, *154*
    Buffalo Pizza, 62–63
    Buffalo Queso, 152
    Buffalo 7-Layer Dip, 143
    Buffalo Stinger Taco, 81–84, *82*
    Cheesy Buffalo Chicken Ring, 136–37, *137*
    Chesterfield-Style Chicken Riggies, 159–61, *161*
    Fried Bologna Sandwich, *67,* 67–68
    Lottie's Pierogi and Buffalo Wing Pierogi, *69,* 70–71
    Mac & , Buffalo Chicken, 117–18
    Oliver's Spinach Loaf, 71–73, *72*
    Pimento, Buffalo Chicken Salad, *150,* 151
    Pizza Logs, *77,* 77–78
    Red Sox Wing Sauce (Garlic Parmesan Hot Wings), 45, *45*
    Sandwich, Buffalo Chicken Grilled, 108–9
    Spaghetti Parm (Meatballs and Sausage Not Included), 79–81, *80*
    Speed Metal Fries, 112–14
    Stuffed Banana Peppers, 84–86, *85*
    Twice-Baked Buffalo Wing Potatoes, *137,* 137–39
    Utica Greens, 165–67, *166*

Chef's Restaurant (Buffalo), 79

Chesterfield Restaurant (Utica), 160, 165

Chicken. *see also* Wings
    Buffalo, Bacon Biscuit Bombs, 129–31
    Buffalo, Grilled Cheese Sandwich, 108–9
    Buffalo, Mac & Cheese, 117–18
    Buffalo, Nachos, 146–47

Buffalo, Parm "Pizza," 147–50, *148*

  Buffalo, Pimento Cheese Salad, *150,* 151

  Buffalo, Pot Pie, *110,* 110–12

  Buffalo, Ring, Cheesy, 136–37, *137*

  Buffalo, Shredded (Instant Pot), 101

  Buffalo, Shredded (Oven-Roasted), 102

  Buffalo, Shredded (Poached/Stovetop), 102

  Buffalo, Shredded (Slow Cooker), 103

  Buffalo, Sloppy Joes (A.K.A. Buffalo Joes), 153–54, *154*

  Buffalo Chip Dip, 155–56, *156*

  Buffalo Fried Rice, *115,* 115–16

  Buffalo Potstickers, 134–35

  Buffalo 7-Layer Dip, 143

  Buffalo Stinger Taco, 81–84, *82*

  Cream of Buffalo Wing Soup, 124–25, *125*

  Finger Sub, *58,* 64–65

  Lottie's Pierogi and Buffalo Wing Pierogi, *69,* 70–71

  Primanti Sandwich, Buffalo-Style, 121–23

  Riggies, Chesterfield-Style, 159–61, *161*

  Robert Baker–Style Cornell Barbecue, *164,* 164–65

  Speed Metal Fries, 112–14

Chocolate, in Sponge Candy, *89,* 89–91

Clinton House (Utica), 159

Clio (Boston), 41

Cocktail, Tom & Jerry, 91–93, *92*

Coleslaw, Buffalo (Buffaslaw), 157

Colosso Taco & Subs (Tonawanda), 81

Cordova, Robert and Jason, 77

Currants, in Pasta con Sarde, *74,* 74–76

D

Daigler, Christopher, 84

Deviled Eggs, Blue Cheese Buffalo, 131–32, *132*

Dips

  Blue Cheese Sour Cream, 95–96

Buffalo Chicken Pimento Cheese Salad, *150,* 151

  Buffalo Chip, 155–56, *156*

  Buffalo Queso, 152

  Buffalo 7-Layer, 143

DiVincenzo, Andy, 84

Doc Sullivan's (Buffalo), 19

Dressing, Homemade Blue Cheese (For Wings), 37–39, *38*

Dwyer's (North Tonawanda), 19

E

Egan, Pierce, 91

Eggs, Deviled, Blue Cheese Buffalo, 131–32, *132*

Elmo's (Getzville), 19–20, 36

Equipment, notes about, 12

F

Falley Allen (Buffalo), 84

Feast of St. Joseph, 76

Fennel, in Pasta con Sarde, *74,* 74–76

Fish

  Buffalo Salmon, 118–19, *119*

  Fry, 65–66

  Pasta con Sarde, *74,* 74–76

Forster, Ed, 81

Fowler, Joe, 89

Frank's Red Hot Sauce

  history of, 22, 39

  making your own, 39–40

Fryer, buying, 12

G

Gemignani, Tony, 61

Gene McCarthy's (Buffalo), 20

Geno, Michael, 159

Grady, Columbus "Marshal," 32–33

Grape Pie, 162–63, *163*

Greens, Utica, 165–67, *166*

H

Horseradish
    about, 52–53
    Beef on Weck Roast Beef, *48,* 51–52
    Easy Beef on Weck, 53–54, *55*
    Easy Homemade, 53
Hot Dog Relish, Ted's, 87
Hot Sauce, Homemade, 39–40

I

Ingredients, notes about, 12

J

Judi's (Niagara Falls), 20

K

Kelly's Korner (Buffalo), 20, 49
Kummelweck Rolls, Homemade, 49–50, *51*

L

Lettuce
    Buffalo Stinger Taco, 81–84, *82*
    Buffalo Wedge Salad, *120,* 120–21
Liaros, Theodore, 87
Lovejoy (Buffalo), 20–21

M

Mammoser's (Hamburg), 21
Mayonnaise, Homemade (and Buffalo Mayo), 100
McCarthy, Jason, 91
Morelle, Joe, 165

N

Nachos, Buffalo Chicken, 146–47
Nine-Eleven Tavern (Buffalo), 21

O

Oliver's Restaurant (Buffalo), 71
Oringer, Ken, 41–42
Ortolani, Thecly, 84

P

Pasta
    Buffalo Chicken Mac & Cheese, 117–18
    Chesterfield-Style Chicken Riggies, 159–61,
        161
    con Sarde, *74,* 74–76
    Spaghetti Parm (Meatballs and Sausage Not
        Included), 79–81, *80*
Pepperoni
    Buffalo Pizza, 62–63
    Pizza Logs, *77,* 77–78
Peppers
    Banana, Stuffed, 84–86, *85*
    Buffalo Chicken Pimento Cheese Salad, *150,*
        151
    Homemade Hot Sauce, 39–40
    Ted's Hot Dog Relish, 87
Pie, Grape, 162–63, *163*
Pierogi
    Lottie's, and Buffalo Wing Pierogi, *69,* 70–71
    at R&L Tavern, 68–69
Pikuzinski, Ronnie and Lottie, 68–69
Pimento Cheese Buffalo Chicken Salad, *150,* 151
Pizza
    Buffalo, 62–63
    Buffalo Chicken Parm, 147–50, *148*
    Buffalo-style, about, 60–61
    Dough, Buffalo, 62
    Logs, *77,* 77–78
    Sauce, Buffalo, 62
The Place (Buffalo), 91
Pok Pok (Brooklyn), 35
Potatoes
    Buffalo Chicken Casserole, 144–45, *145*
    Fish Fry, 65–66
    Lottie's Pierogi and Buffalo Wing Pierogi, *69,*
        70–71
    Primanti Sandwich, Buffalo-Style, 121–23
    Speed Metal Fries, 112–14
    Twice-Baked Buffalo Wing, *137,* 137–39

Pot Pie, Buffalo Chicken, *110*, 110–12
Potstickers, Buffalo, 134–35
Primanti Bros. (Pittsburgh, PA), 121

R

Recipes, notes about, 12
Redwood Restaurant (Naples, NY), 162
Relish, Ted's Hot Dog, 87
Rice, Buffalo Fried, *115*, 115–16
Ricker, Andy, 35
R&L (Buffalo), 68–69
Rolls, Homemade Kummelweck, 49–50, *51*
Romano, Pat, 112

S

Salads
    Buffalo Chicken Pimento Cheese, *150*, 151
    Buffalo Wedge, *120*, 120–21
Salmon, Buffalo, 118–19, *119*
Sandwiches
    beef on weck, about, 56–57
    Beef on Weck Roast Beef, *48*, 51–52
    Buffalo Chicken Grilled Cheese, 108–9
    Buffalo Chicken Sloppy Joes (A.K.A. Buffalo Joes),
        153–54, *154*
    Chicken Finger Sub, *58*, 64–65
    Easy Beef on Weck, 53–54, *55*
    Fried Bologna, *67*, 67–68
    Primanti, Buffalo-Style, 121–23
Sardines, in Pasta con Sarde, *74*, 74–76
Sauces. *see also* Wing Sauces
    Frank's Red Hot, history of, 22, 39
    Hot, Homemade, 39–40
Schenk, Monica, 162
Shrimp, Buffalo Rock, with Blue Cheese Tempura,
    133–34, *134*
Sloppy Joes, Buffalo Chicken (A.K.A. Buffalo Joes),
    153–54, *154*
Soup, Cream of Buffalo Wing, 124–25, *125*
Sour Cream, Blue Cheese, 95–96

Speed Metal Fries, 112–14
Spellman, Adam, 160 .
Spinach Loaf, Oliver's, 71–73, *72*
Sponge Candy, *89*, 89–91

T

Taco, Buffalo Stinger, 81–84, *82*
Talde, Dale, 25–27
Ted's (Buffalo), 87
Ted's Hot Dog Relish, 87
Thomas, Dave, 79
Thomas, Jerry, 91
Tick Tock Diner (Clifton, NJ), 112
Tomatoes
    Buffalo Queso, 152
    Buffalo Stinger Taco, 81–84, *82*
    Buffalo Wedge Salad, *120*, 120–21
    Chesterfield-Style Chicken Riggies, 159–61, *161*
Tom & Jerry Cocktail, 91–93, *92*
Tortillas and tortilla chips
    Buffalo Chicken Nachos, 146–47
    Buffalo Chip Dip, 155–56, *156*
    Buffalo Stinger Taco, 81–84, *82*

U

Utica Greens, 165–67, *166*

W

Waffles, Buttermilk, Buffalo Wings and Blue Cheese,
    105–8, *106*
Whirl
    about, 46–47
    Wing Sauce, 47
Wiechec's (Kaisertown), 21, 44
Wings
    best frying oil for, 35
    Buffalo, and Blue Cheese Buttermilk Waffles,
        105–8, *106*
    Buffalo, Baked, 28–30, *30*
    Buffalo, favorite spots for, 18–21

Wings (*continued*)

    Buffalo, Off-the-Pit BBQ, *43,* 44

    Buffalo, Old-School, 23–24

    Chef Andy Ricker on, 35

    Chef Dale Talde on, 25–27

    Chef José Andrés on, 31

    Chef Ken Oringer on, 41–42

    Chef Marshal Grady's Bleu Bayou, *32,* 32–34

    cooking techniques, 23

Elmo's Cajun-Barbecue, 36–37

    recipe history, 17

Wing Sauces

    Buffalo, 22

    Homemade Blue Cheese Dressing (For Wings), 37–39, *38*

    Red Sox (Garlic Parmesan Hot Wings), 45, *45*

    Spicy Blue Cheese Buffalo Sauce, 46

    Whirl, 47